BERLITZ

CRETE

1991/1992 Edition

By the staff of Berlitz Guides

Copyright © 1990, 1977 by Berlitz Publishing S.A.,
Avenue d'Ouchy 61, 1000 Lausanne 6, Switzerland.

All rights reserved. No part of this book may be reproduced or transmitted in any form or by any means, electronic or mechanical, including photocopying, recording or by any information storage and retrieval system without permission in writing from the publisher.

Berlitz Trademark Reg. U.S. Patent Office and other countries. Marca Registrada. Library of Congress Catalog Card No. 76-21369.

Printed in Switzerland by Weber S.A., Bienne.

**18th Printing
1991/1992 Edition**

Updated or revised 1990, 1988, 1986, 1985, 1984, 1983, 1982, 1981, 1980, 1979, 1978

How to use our guide

- All the practical information, hints and tips that you will need before and during the trip start on page 97.

- For general background, see the sections The Island and the People, p. 6, and A Brief History, p. 12.

- All the sights to see are listed between pages 23 and 71. Our own choice of sights most highly recommended is pinpointed by the Berlitz traveller symbol.

- Entertainment, nightlife and all other leisure activities are described between pages 72 and 87, while information on restaurants and cuisine is to be found on pages 88 to 96.

- Finally, there is an index at the back of the book, pp. 126–128.

Found an error or an omission in this Berlitz Guide? Or a change or new feature we should know about? Our editor would be happy to hear from you, and a postcard would do. Be sure to include your name and address, since in appreciation for a useful suggestion, we'd like to send you a free travel guide.

Although we make every effort to ensure the accuracy of all the information in this book, changes occur incessantly. We cannot therefore take responsibility for facts, prices, addresses and circumstances in general that are constantly subject to alteration.

Text: Michael Laurence
Photography: Luc Chessex
We are very grateful to the Greek National Tourist Organization for its valuable assistance in the preparation of this book. We would also like to thank Christina Papavasilopoulou, Evangelos Vrentzos, Jim Bennett and Justin Lee for their help in revising and updating this edition of our guide.
Cartography: Falk-Verlag, Hamburg.

Contents

The Island and the People		6
A Brief History		12
Where to Go		23
	Iráklion	24
	Knossós	32
	Górtis, Phaistós and Agía Triáda	40
	Eastern Crete	45
	Western Crete	53
	Excursions	64
What to Do		
	Music and Dance	72
	Museums and Archaeological Sites	75
	Shopping	76
Sports and Outdoor Activities		80
Wining and Dining		88
Blueprint for a Perfect Trip (Practical Information)		97
Index		126

Maps

Bird's-Eye View of Crete	6
Iráklion	25
Knossós	33
Eastern Crete	46
Western Crete	54
Chaniá	57

The Island and the People

> There is a land called Crete in the midst of the wine-dark sea.
>
> Homer, *The Odyssey*

Crete's long and legendary history has created an aura about the island. This is where European civilization began with the dazzling Minoans who flourished between 3000 and 1400 B.C. and then disappeared in mysterious circumstances, but not without leaving behind magnificent palaces filled with extraordinary artefacts.

Knossós, Phaistós, Mália, Káto Zákros—these opulent vestiges of the Minoan culture evoke a fascinating world of long, long ago. For over 3,000 years, the splendid ruins lay buried under the rich, Cretan soil. Then, at the turn of the century, Sir Arthur Evans unearthed and vividly reconstructed the Minoan splendour at Knossós. The discovery of other palaces followed, but none as grand as Knossós.

This is where the myth of the labyrinth and the mino-

taur originated. The past starts to come alive as you follow the elaborate passageways, past blood-red columns into the heart of the Minoan world. Fresco-lined corridors take you into royal chambers, out onto balconies overlooking the countryside and back through intricately connected rooms, lined with sacred double axes and bulls' horns. The ruins reveal an astonishingly sophisticated civilization—with a plumbing system unequalled until modern times.

In the verdant Great Plain of Messará lie the lyrical ruins of the palace of Phaistós. Not as thoroughly restored as Knossós, this large palace blends well into its setting. Other smaller palaces and entire Minoan villages are scattered all over the island.

Current critics question whether Evans was justified in his fairytale-like re-creation of the Minoan civilization. Were these palaces, perhaps, huge necropolises like the labyrinthine tombs of the Egyptians? The Minoans themselves are much in evidence in the well-preserved frescoes: elegant, beautiful people who seem to spend their time in exotic play. But as you wander through the ruins of the complicated palaces the

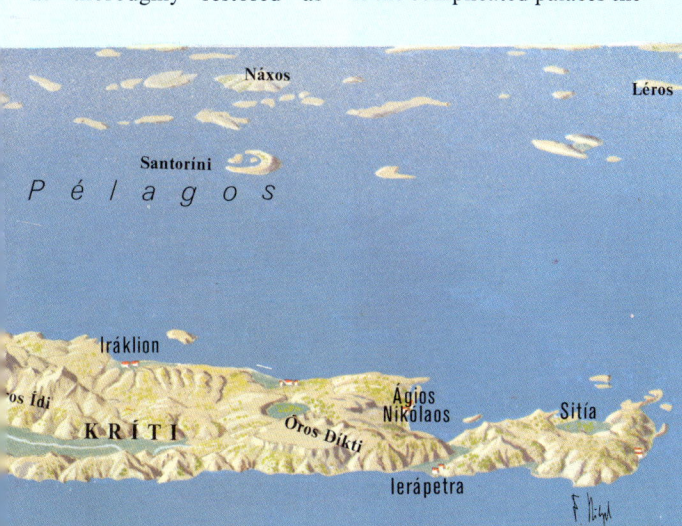

mystery of the Minoans deepens rather than unravels.

Crete abounds in other mythology as well. It is said that Zeus, father of the gods, was born and brought up in the mountain caves here. You can momentarily join the gods today by climbing to these caves on Mount Díkti and Mount Ídi. And Europe got its name from Princess Europa, who also figures in a Cretan legend. Abducted from her royal palace in Phoenicia by Zeus, disguised as a bull, the princess was taken to Crete, where she became the mother of King Minos.

Over the centuries, this island—equidistant from North Africa, the Middle East and Europe—has been ruled by many nations who prized its ideal location. The Minoans ruled Crete for over a millennium and a half. Later, the Romans and the Saracen Arabs dominated the island. The Venetians governed for 400 years and the Turks for over 200 years. The visible reminders of Crete's varied history include the Minoan sites, Venetian forts and elegant houses and the exotic East's mosques and minarets. Only in 1913 did Crete officially become part of Greece.

Trade developed thanks to its position in the Mediterranean Sea. The Minoans maintained a vast maritime empire and traded to the four corners of the known world. Crete was long famous abroad for its wines, olive oil and honey. But the ships sailing to and from Crete today have a more lucrative cargo... tourists.

Cretan pottery styled on classic lines is always in great demand.

Willing young models pose for snapshots; right: vast Kastélli Bay in the island's north-west corner.

The island is ringed with beaches and harbours and criss-crossed with dramatic mountains. Between the mountains and the sea are seemingly endless olive groves and vineyards, orchards and orange plantations, with their blossoms scenting the air and their products filling the markets. Although the mountains are snow-capped in winter, the temperature at sea level never falls below freezing and flowers bloom all year long.

Busy Iráklion, once the headquarters of piracy and slave trading in the Mediterranean, is a modern tourist centre in the middle of Crete. The Venetian wall still rings Iráklion, and its streets follow their medieval plan.

The eastern half of Crete's north coast has been developed for tourism in recent years. Its mild climate, picturesque towns and Minoan sites make this Cretan Riviera especially attractive. The popular harbour towns of Réthimnon and Chaniá to the west, with their Venetian and Turkish overtones, have fine beaches.

In the rugged Sfakiá Mountains, life has remained essentially unchanged for hundreds of years. You'll see the Sfakiot men here with their great moustaches, wearing tall boots, baggy blue pantaloons and colourfully embroidered waistcoats over black shirts— the Cretan national costume.

Crete's size, independence and relative isolation make it almost a separate continent. An early tourist (1609) referred to it as "Queene of the Isles Mediterrene". Even the Greeks call it the Great Island. Miles and miles of beaches, rugged mountains and tangible remnants of history make Crete an island of never-ending variety. Here the past is as alive as the very lively present. And, despite centuries of foreign influence, Crete remains resolutely Cretan.

Who but these fiercely independent islanders would name their sons *Elefthérios* (freedom)? There is an old Greek proverb that two Cretans equal an argument. This would seem to have been the case throughout the centuries—except when their independence has been threatened. Then it's a united front, fervently Cretan.

Crete's splendid climate is matched by the warmth of the local hospitality. Don't be surprised if a shopkeeper sends out for coffee for you while you browse or if you're offered the gift of an orange or a flower in a village. It's all part of being a *xénos* (which means both stranger and guest) on the historic island of Crete.

A Brief History

While the rest of the world was still in the Stone Age, migrants from Anatolia (Asia Minor), Egypt and Libya began a new civilization in Crete. This sophisticated culture, now called Minoan after King Minos and his descendants, lasted from approximately 3000 to 1400 B.C. At the peak of their golden age, the Minoans no doubt considered their European counterparts total barbarians.

References to this ancient civilization on Crete appear in *The Odyssey:* Homer mentions "The mighty city of Knossós wherein Minos ruled". But we owe most of our knowledge of the Minoans to one adventurous man—British archaeologist Sir Arthur Evans. With vision, industry and his own money he partly reconstructed the great palace of Knossós, rediscovering the

Minoan world. Though other Minoan palaces and even complete towns have been unearthed, none of these equals the scope of Evans' Knossós.

Some of Sir Arthur's reconstructed history has recently been questioned. One current theory is that the palaces were actually spacious burial quarters for dead Minoans, something like the Egyptian tombs. But a complete explanation of Minoan life remains as elusive as the solution of their mythological labyrinth.

The surviving frescoes and drawings on pottery provide vivid clues to a very colourful society. We know, for example, that the Minoans were a physically strong and graceful people, though rarely more than five feet tall. We know how they dressed: the men in brief loincloths, ornamental cod-pieces and sandals; the women, bare-breasted, in exotic, full-length dresses. Both sexes went in for elaborate hair styles and brilliant, fanciful jewellery.

The Minoans were prosperous, peaceful, given to sumptuous living and spectacular, often cruel, sacred ceremonies. Somewhere between sport and religion, and shrouded in legend, is the Minoan version of bullfighting, bull-leaping. The bulls' horns decorating the palaces indicate that the Minoans took it every bit as seriously as the Spanish. Statues and frescoes (such as the ivory acrobat figure and *Toreador* fresco in the Iráklion museum) lead us to believe that unarmed young men and women confronted specially

In such a setting, it's easy to understand how myths were born.

consecrated, mammoth bulls in an arena. They faced the charging bull and at the crucial moment grasped its horns and somersaulted agilely over the bull's head onto its back and then to the ground again. Of course, there was always the chance of being split open like a ripe fig. Afterwards, the bull would be sacrificed under the edge of gigantic double axes.

These axes, a predominant Minoan motif, are intertwined with other elements of the culture. The word *labyrinth* probably comes from the pre-Hellenic *labrys* (double axe). A clay tablet found in Knossós mentions an important cult figure called the Lady of the Labyrinth who lived in the House of the Double Axes, in other words, within Knossós.

The Minoan legend of the labyrinth and the minotaur is simply the age-old story of a hero who overcomes a dark and hidden evil with the aid of a princess who loves him. The Minoan version begins with King Minos' wife, Queen Pasiphaë, giving birth to a half-man, half-beast—the minotaur—after a dalliance with a sacred bull. King Minos has his chief architect, the famous Daedalus, design a labyrinth to contain the creature. Every nine years a group of young Athenians are sacrificed to the minotaur, but when Theseus, son of the King of Athens, arrives with the victims, King Minos' daughter, Ariadne, falls in love with him. The princess gives Theseus a ball of twine to unwind in the labyrinth so that he can find his

Perhaps a priestess, this elegant Minoan is known as La Parisienne.

way out again. After slaying the evil minotaur and emerging from the labyrinth, Theseus claims Ariadne and returns triumphant to Athens. This particular love story does not have a happy ending. On the way back to Athens, Theseus ungallantly leaves Ariadne behind on the island of Náxos and later becomes entangled with another famous Cretan, Phaedra.

Mary Renault, in her novel *The King Must Die,* suggests that Theseus' triumph precipitated the destruction of Minoan culture. How much of this powerful legend is based on reality is a Minoan mystery

A Knossós fresco vividly depicts the perilous art of bull-leaping.

which continues to tantalize visitors to Crete.

The Minoans were known as a great naval power in the Mediterranean. The vast cypress forests that covered the island in those days provided the raw material for their boats. A commercial rather than a military power, Crete was extremely well situated between two continents. The Minoans traded and forged links with all the surrounding countries. Their rich land produced enough wine, olive oil and honey for export. Copper and tin were imported to make bronze, some of which was then traded abroad. For their jewellery, the Minoans obtained lapis lazuli from Afghanistan, ivory from Syria, and gold, silver and black obsidian from west Anatolia (now part of Turkey). Recently discovered artefacts indicate that the Minoans may have sailed through the Straits of Gibraltar and as far to the north as Scandinavia. They were definitely in Egypt. Three-thousand-year-old murals in Egyptian tombs show processions of Keftiu (as the Cretans were called), which resemble those found at Knossós.

At their height, the Minoans numbered several million, about four times more than today, and the population of Knossós was around 100,000. The written language, a form of hieroglyphics or pictographs, has been found on thousands of clay tablets. Possibly based on an Indo-European or Semitic language, it has been called Linear A. The language which supplanted Linear A in about 1500 B.C.—and became, of course, Linear B—has been identified as an early form of Greek. Unfortunately most of the existing bits of hieroglyphics are not at all literary, but rather what we might term "grocery lists". The spiral design of the lovely and curious Phaistós Disc in the Iráklion museum has inspired many interpretations, but no one yet has deciphered its message.

About halfway through the Minoan era, an earthquake occurred. The Minoans rebuilt and rose to even greater heights. The ruins we see now date mainly from the period after the earthquake.

How and why did this brilliant civilization end? Evans and others suppose a cataclysmic ending, perhaps connected with the volcanic eruption on the island of Santoríni (Thera) to the north in 1450 B.C., followed by tremendous earthquakes and probably invasions. Other theories mention a religious decline, in particular an obsession with the dead, which eventually transformed the great palaces into abandoned mausoleums. It's doubtful that the Minoans suddenly ceased to exist. New evidence (and, naturally, new theories) continually comes to light, and the future may find the undiscovered answers to the mysterious disappearance of the Minoans.

Dorians, Romans and Saracen Arabs

After the Minoan era, Crete slipped into obscurity. Its commercial powers declined. Tall, blond Dorians from the north-western Balkans over-ran the island. The only major feature surviving from the period preceding the Roman

Message of Phaistós Disc remains undeciphered; below: Górtina's Roman Odeon with its Law Code.

Time-honoured Cretan technique for getting olives out of the trees.

occupation is a Code of Laws incised on stone at Górtis (or Górtina; see p. 40).

The Romans came to Crete as arbiters—to settle long years of internal struggles —and stayed on as governors (from 67 B.C. to A.D. 395). They made Górtis their capital and, in their usual fashion, built roads, temples, villas and aqueducts.

St. Paul arrived at Kalí Liménes on the south coast in A.D. 59, bringing Christianity to Crete. When the Roman empire divided into western and eastern factions, Crete became part of Byzantium under the aegis of the patriarchate of Constantinople. The Cretans remained Christian through the later Arab occupations.

In the 9th century, the Saracen Arabs conquered Crete. Led by Abu Hafs Omar, they turned the island into a piracy base, making it a major slave market in the Mediterranean. They also established a fort, Rabd-el-Kandek, which later became the city of Iráklion. When the Byzantines liberated Crete in 961, they renamed the fort Chandax. The Byzantine general is said to have catapulted the captured Muslims' heads into the fort. Those Muslims who kept their heads became slaves.

Under the Venetians and Turks
During the Fourth Crusade, Byzantium fell and Crete was sold for cash to Venice. Thus began 465 years of Venetian occupation (1204–1669). But the Cretans—never a people to take foreign rule lightly—fiercely maintained their individuality, initiating many bloody revolutions. The Cretans—also not a people to ignore foreigners—intermarried with the occupying forces as the years went by and, eventually, participated in the government. The Venetians renamed the city of Chandax Candia, extending the name to the whole island (mistakenly called "Candy" by Shakespeare and several other European writers).

Crete thrived under the Venetians. It was a period of great public building. The harbour and the fortifications of Iráklion still stand, prominently displaying the Lion of St. Mark. The island even had its own Renaissance during the 16th and 17th centuries. The greatest local literary figure of the era, Vitsénzos Kornáros, is known for his long, heroic work in Cretan dialect, *Erotókritos*. It's so familiar on the island that mountain villagers can recite portions of it from memory.

Better known internationally are the painters of the Cretan Renaissance. When Constantinople fell to the Turks in 1453, innumerable artists sought refuge in Crete. The Venetian and Byzantine heritage combined with the dynamic Cretan style to forge a powerful school of painting. Two of its greatest artists were Michaíl Damaskinós—best represented by six icons in the Church of St. Catherine in Iráklion—and Domínikos Theotokópoulos, who later signed his works "The Greek", in Spanish "El Greco". Many lesser artists were also active in Crete during this period. Though time and carelessness have caused some damage, you can see icons and frescoes from this period glowing in the dimly lit interiors of 800 churches and chapels scattered over the island.

The Battle for Crete

The Venetians prized Crete for its productivity and its important location. In the mid-17th century, when the Ottoman empire began to expand, the Venetians recognized that Crete was the last bastion of Christianity, the last barrier on the road to the West. When the famous Turkish pirate Barbarossa Khair ed-Din scored a minor victory against Crete, the Venetians began strengthening their fortifications. It was because of these improvements that they were able to hold out for so long. In the end, the Turks took Chaniá (1645) and then Réthimnon. Three years later, the Turks began their assault on the capital of Candia. After 15 years of fruitless siege, the Turkish commander, Hussein Pasha, was summoned back to Constantinople where he was publicly strangled for his failure to take the city. The Turks doubled their efforts, waging one of the longest battles of its kind in history: 21 years.

Historians estimate that over 30,000 Venetians and 118,000 Turks lost their lives. When the rest of Europe finally came to Venice's aid, it was too late. Candia fell to the Turks. As they strode in through the city's main gates, the Venetians fled with their most precious possession, the head of St. Titus, the island's patron saint (which has only recently been returned to Crete). The Turks settled in for an occupation of 200 years (1669–1898).

Crete slid back into the dark ages. The pashas' rule was both exacting and indolent. They allowed culture, the buildings and the island itself to deteriorate. These were years of violent revolutions. When Greece rose up against the Ottoman empire on the mainland in the 19th century, Crete followed suit. Always known for their independence of spirit and their ferocity, the Cretans declared they wanted "freedom or death".

Into the 20th Century

In 1897, a coalition of European powers (Great Britain, France, Russia and Italy) expelled the Turks and briefly took the island's affairs in hand. During this period, a young woman of dubious reputation from Marseilles appeared in Crete. This colourful character was later immortalized as Madame Hortense in Níkos Kazantzákis' novel *Zorba*. The admirals of the nations all wined and dined her aboard their ships anchored in Soúda Bay. Stories relate that she could remember each admiral in the morning by his scent: cologne for the English admiral, violet for the French, musk for the Russian and *patchouli* for the Italian. When the great powers left, "Madame Hortense" was rowed ashore and saluted with a round of cannon-fire.

The European powers forced the Turks to give Crete autonomous status within the Ottoman empire and to accept Prince George, second son of the Greek king, as governor. Under the new régime, the name of the main city was changed again—this time to Iráklion, after ancient Heraklia.

Greece's great statesman, Elefthérios Venizélos, came from Crete. He rose to prominence at the beginning of the century with his campaign for *énosis,* union with Greece. This eventually came about in 1913, after a coalition of

Huge clay jars at Knossós site; below, bust of Sir Arthur Evans, who unearthed them.

Off in search of a secluded beach or cove, often inaccessible by land.

Greeks, Serbians, Montenegrins and Bulgarians defeated the Turks.

Crete was also in the news at this time because of Sir Arthur Evans' remarkable discoveries at Knossós. Other excavators brought more publicity to this already well-known island. The Cretans set about rebuilding, and they prospered as they developed their agricultural resources and attracted tourists with the newly discovered sites.

The year 1923 marked the final evacuation of Turks from Crete. The 10,000 Turks who had previously chosen to remain on Crete were exchanged for 13,000 Greek refugees from Asia Minor.

Decades passed in peace and growing prosperity for Crete. But in 1941 disaster struck. The rapid advance of the Germans in Greece forced the Allied forces to retreat to Crete. Then, in a ten-day battle, British, Australian and New Zealand soldiers joined the Cretans in a valiant attempt to defend the island against airborne attack. Though the Germans won, it was an expensive victory. During the occupation that ensued, many Cretans carried on guerrilla warfare and managed to survive under harsh conditions.

When the war was over in 1945, much of Crete was in ruins from bombing. Unlike the mainland, it did manage to avoid the post-war disaster of civil war. Slowly, Crete has regained its reputation as the "Great Island", an ideal holiday place, steeped in history and characterized by hospitality.

Where to Go

Whether you come by sea or air, Iráklion will most likely be your first view of Crete. It's centrally located, of major archaeological interest and well worth a day or two of sightseeing. It's possible to see the city's high points—the Archaeological Museum and the ruins of nearby Knossós—in a very full day. But then you'd be missing the best of Crete.

Most tourists don't choose bustling Iráklion for their headquarters but head for the charming old harbour towns of Chaniá or Réthimnon, or for one of the modern resorts sprouting up along the sandy beaches of the north-east and south coasts.

A rented car is the ideal way to explore Crete. With your own transport, you can discover the less obvious attractions and do it at your own pace. If you don't want to get involved in driving, there are innumerable guided tours and a vast network of bus routes that will take you to all but the most inaccessible places. However you decide to go around Crete, you'll rarely be out of sight of the sea and miles and miles of beaches.

Iráklion
Pop. 102,000

In the midst of all its busy city life, Iráklion has a number of interesting and endearing features. One is the Venetian harbour—a good place to begin a tour of the city.

The sunlight is intense here, reflecting off the blue water and the white cargo ships. The new outer harbour bustles with ferries and freighters, but the inner harbour is for fishing boats, yachts and caïques. To the east, you can see Día, a small, barren island named after one of Zeus' many nymph friends, said to have been cast there by Hera, Zeus' jealous wife.

The top attraction in Iráklion is the **Venetian castle,** still known by its Turkish name *(Koúles)*. Though it's now a museum, it still fulfils anyone's notion of a romantic castle. The enormously thick, gold-stone walls of the fortress, built between 1523 and 1549, are pierced by arched windows; from the battlements you have a fine view of the harbour and the sea. History echoes within its walls. In the 17th century, the Venetians waged a 21-year, ultimately unsuccessful, battle to hold on to the fort. On three of

It's Greek to Me

Finding your way around in Crete is facilitated by the local practice of subtitling many Greek road signs with a version in the Latin alphabet, the form generally adopted in this guide. But watch out: the Greeks themselves don't always agree, and you will come across various spellings of the same word. For instance, the town of Χανιά may appear as Chaniá, Xaniá, Haniá or even Khaniá.

In the case of well-known sites (like Athens and Crete) and proper names in a historical or literary context, we've used the time-honoured English spelling.

Stress, a very important feature of the Greek language, is indicated by an accent mark (´) over the vowel of the syllable to be emphasized.

Two words you'll want to learn immediately are ΠΛΑΤΕΙΑ *(platía)*, meaning square, and ΟΔΟΣ *(odós)*, meaning street.

For more about modern Greek spelling and pronunciation, see ALPHABET in the Blueprint section of this book.

the outside walls you can still see the sculptured lions of St. Mark. The best one is on the seaward side.

Slightly less important are the huge arcades and storerooms of the 16th-century *arsenali,* located on the quay across the street from the harbour authority. These vaulted tunnels and rooms were once used for building and repairing ships.

From the harbour, you can walk around the **Venetian walls** encircling the city. The promenade, about 2½ miles in length, affords a dramatic and panoramic view of Iráklion. Built in the 15th century, enlarged during the 16th and 17th, the walls are mainly in good condition. At the southern end, you will find a small zoo and very pleasant gardens. The highest point is the **Promachón Martinéngo,** burial place of Cretan novelist Níkos Kazantzákis. The impressive stone marking his grave carries the poignant message: "I hope for nothing. I fear nothing. I am free."

Three gateways, cutting through the Venetian walls, reveal a thickness of 60 feet. The main gate, the Pantokrátor, is now known as the Chanióporta, because the main road to Chánia and points west begins here. In the area outside this gate is the bus station for Phaistós, Mátala, Agía Galíni and villages to the south.

When you feel the need for a break from wall walking, go to **Platía Venizélou** (known locally as Lions' Square), near the end of the busy Odós 25 Avgoú-

stou, which climbs straight from the harbour. In the centre of this triangular square stands the **Morosini Fountain** (1628), named after a Venetian governor-general. The four 14th-century lions supporting the fountain were taken from an earlier fountain. A delightful and sporting crowd of nymphs, bulls, dolphins and musicians frolic across the

16th-century Venetian castle guards entrance to Iráklion harbour.

bas-reliefs of the lower basins. Though hardly in the realm of artistic chefs d'œuvre, this charming fountain provides an interesting focal point for the square.

Take a seat at one of the outdoor cafés in the square, order coffee and a custard-filled pastry *(bougátsa)* and enjoy the scene. White-coated waiters with silver trays hurry about and traffic spins past, while the Cretans at other tables are settling political questions and arranging marriages at the usual Mediterranean pace over their tiny cups of coffee or *oúzo*. The square has a good supply of souvenir shops and bookshops that carry international newspapers and magazines.

Across from the fountain stands the **Basilica of Ágios Márkos** (St. Mark). It was built under the Venetians in 1239, rebuilt after an earthquake in 1303, repaired after a second earthquake in 1508, turned into a mosque under the Turks and finally restored to its Venetian character in the 1960s. The basilica's greatest attraction is a series of repro-

Iráklion's cathedral, one of three churches on Platía Agías Ekaterínis.

ductions of 13th-, 14th- and 15th-century frescoes from Cretan churches. Many of the originals are almost inaccessible to the average tourist. But, the reproductions should inspire an effort to see the originals of the more easily reached frescoes. (In general admission is free. However, when there's a special exhibition a small fee is charged.)

Back a few paces on Odós 25 Avgoústou, you will find the Church of **Ágios Títos,** the patron saint of Crete. Each occupying power built onto the original Greek Byzantine church, concocting an architectural medley of the island's history. Inside, you can see a reliquary of the head of St. Titus. When the Turks occupied Crete, it was sent to Venice for safe keeping and wasn't returned until 1966.

Nearby, El Greco Park has two welcome features, especially for parents: a children's playground and lavatory facilities.

Beyond Platía Venizélou runs Leofóros Kalokerinoú, once the Venetian Via Imperialis. It's still a busy thoroughfare for a multitude of shopping tastes. Nearby, Platía Agías Ekaterínis contains the 19th-century cathedral of Iráklion.

Next to it is the small, far more charming church of Ágios Minás, dating from the previous century. But the real reason for coming to the square is to see a third church, **Agía Ekateríni** (St. Catherine's), built in the 16th century, enhanced a century later with such features as the beautiful entry. It harbours a fine collection of frescoes, carvings and other art from Cretan churches. The highlight is six **icons** by Michaíl Damaskinós, painted between 1580 and 1590. Opulent, extravagant, visionary and haunting, these works blend Byzantine conventions and Renaissance inspiration with a Cretan vigour. Damaskinós, a contemporary of El Greco, is considered the second greatest painter of Crete.

When you're tired of churches and history, stroll over to the **market,** located on Odós 1866. Let your eyes and nose direct you to this exotic bazaar of speciality stalls and enticing food. But don't sample too many of the various white cheeses and black olives, because the experience of eating excellent and authentic Cretan food awaits you in the narrow street between the market and Odós Évans. This is the place to go in

Colourful display of local produce in Iráklion's busy central market.

Iráklion to enjoy a good meal. As in all Cretan restaurants, you should go directly into the kitchen to choose what you want. Language is no problem here—just point a finger at the desired dishes.

The market street goes into Platía Kornárou and the 16th-century Bembo Fountain with its headless Roman statue. The souvenir kiosk beyond looks like a Turkish fountain. It once was.

Leofóros Vasiléos Konstantínou (now officially called Leofóros Dikeosýnis), with its many fine shops, ends in Platía Eleftherías, where all of Iráklion takes its evening promenade or *vólta*. The huge square contains outdoor cafés, cinemas and the Archaeological Museum. On Sundays there are occasionally band concerts.

Not so mammoth you need Ariadne's thread to find your way around, the **Archaeological Museum** *(Archeologikó Mousío)* is a well-lighted, well-displayed treasure trove of the world's greatest collection of Minoan artefacts. Many of the tags are in English, but if you want a comprehensive explanation, buy the museum's official guide book.

The collection starts with the Neolithic Period and ends with the great Minoan frescoes. Ideally, one should visit the museum first, go to the sites and then return a second time here to round out the picture. The majority of the artefacts come from Knossós, Phaistós, Agía Triáda, Mália and the palace of Káto Zákros. The museum does not overwhelm the visitor: it's a collection of the Minoans' everyday utensils and ornaments, their sacred figures and frescoes—though the gigantic double axes are certainly awesome.

One of the museum's highlights is the **Phaistós Disc,** with its mysterious message spiralling towards the centre. See, too, the charmingly carved ivory acrobat, the *Bull-Jumper,* and the earthenware plaques known as the *Town Mosaic.* Resembling flattened children's blocks, each bears the façade of a Minoan house. The best of Minoan art is represented by the *Chieftain's Cup,* the *Harvester's Vase* and the *Athlete's* (or *Boxer's*) *Vase,* which depict important events in Minoan life.

The upper floor of the museum contains several famous frescoes—the almond-eyed Minoan woman, known as **La Parisienne,** and the *Prince of the Lilies.* Here you will see the acrobatic bull-leapers and the *Saffron Gatherer,* which in its original restoration was assumed to be a boy but was later discovered to be a

Rugged mountain dweller remains unaffected by tourist invasion.

monkey. Many of these frescoes depict flowers and plants, especially lilies and irises, that you find in every Cretan garden today.

The most valuable piece in all the collection is a **sarcophagus** from Agía Triáda, also on the second floor. Made of painted limestone, this 3,300-year-old tomb has fascinating paintings on its sides showing religious rituals.

On the other side of Iráklion, across from the Xenía Hotel, is the **Historical Museum** *(Istorikó Mousío)*. It picks up where the Archaeological Museum leaves off, covering the Early Christian, Byzantine, Venetian and Turkish periods. Highlights here are reconstructions of a typical Cretan peasant's house from the late 1800s and the study of novelist Níkos Kazantzákis with his work desk, library, photographs and personal objects.

Iráklion has some well-maintained but busy beaches around it. The nearest, and most crowded, is FLORIDA BEACH *(Karterós);* the beach run by the EOT (National Tourist Organization) has all the amenities. Both are reached by bus from Iráklion, as are the miles of beaches all along the coast to the east.

Knossós
(Iráklion, 5 km.)

Entering Knossós under an arcade of bougainvillea, you come to a bronze bust of Sir Arthur Evans, the man who discovered and reconstructed Knossós and the Minoan world.

Though historical references to the site abounded, it was not until 1878 that an amateur archaeologist from Crete—with the appropriate name of Mínos Kalokairinós—unearthed the palace's storerooms. The ruling Turkish authorities soon put a stop to his work, but the discovery caught the attention of the eccentric German archaeologist Heinrich Schliemann. Having uncovered Troy and the Mycenaean civilizations on the mainland, he came to Crete expecting further Mycenaean revelations. Unfortunately, Schliemann's parsimonious nature prevented his success: he quarrelled over the price of the land—and even over the number of olive trees growing there—and left Crete, disappointed, in 1886. Eight years later Sir Arthur Evans arrived in search of linguistic tablets and seal (engraved) stones.

Evans had money, energy,

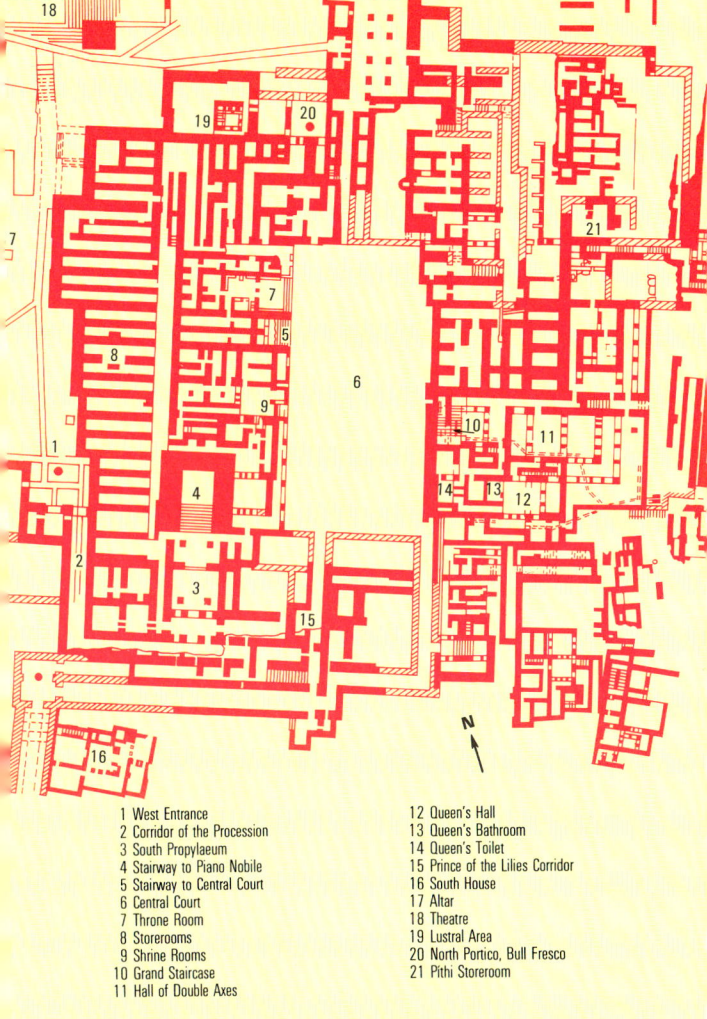

1 West Entrance
2 Corridor of the Procession
3 South Propylaeum
4 Stairway to Piano Nobile
5 Stairway to Central Court
6 Central Court
7 Throne Room
8 Storerooms
9 Shrine Rooms
10 Grand Staircase
11 Hall of Double Axes
12 Queen's Hall
13 Queen's Bathroom
14 Queen's Toilet
15 Prince of the Lilies Corridor
16 South House
17 Altar
18 Theatre
19 Lustral Area
20 North Portico, Bull Fresco
21 Pithi Storeroom

vision and luck. Even world politics was on his side. The Turks had been chased out of Greece and archaeologists were allowed considerable freedom. Evans bought the hillside in the Kaíratos Valley and, while searching for seal stones and pictograph clay tablets, found the Palace of Minos. From 1900 to 1940, he dedicated his life to the colossal task of excavating and reconstructing the palace.

Your first view of Knossós may be less than impressive. But this is typical of the palace of King Minos: you enter in the least dramatic way and the spectacle unfolds slowly.

Don't expect your route through Knossós to follow a straight line. The approximately 1,200 rooms form a labyrinth of deliberate perplexity. Before reaching the heart of the palace, a massive central court, you are likely to follow a number of false routes. And once in the central court, a flight of stairs seemingly leading out will send you back into the sunlight-filled court. Was all this complexity a protection against enemies and evil spirits? If the Minoan palaces were mausoleums, as has been suggested, were their complicated patterns part of sacred rituals? Or did the labyrinth, created by the master craftsman Daedalus, merely reflect the Minoan sense of play? In any event, the exploring tourist can now find his way around the reconstructed palace without too much difficulty.

The long, 10-foot-wide corridor leading into the palace is lined with frescoes, restored by the Gilliérons, the Swiss father and son who did so much to recreate Minoan art at Knossós. The frescoes in this **Corridor of the Procession** show two Minoans with their dark skin, short loin cloths and curly black hair. Marching toward the centre of the palace, they carry vessels, just as the real Minoans did.

A slight detour off the corridor brings you to the 6-foot-tall **Horns of Consecration,** which perfectly frame a view of Mount Gioúktas. The curving proportions of the sacred horns have also cradled a succession of smiling tourists.

Past the horns and the partially restored South Propylaeum (containing a replica of

Partly reconstructed, the palace of King Minos at Knossós evokes the splendours of that ancient court.

the *Cup Bearer* fresco), you come not to the expected central court but to a flight of broad stairs leading to the upper storey, or *piano nobile*. The walls here contain reproductions of frescoes. From the balcony you can look down on the **central court** (174 feet long and 87 feet wide), which can be reached by several entrances. Facing south, ceremonial rooms go off to the right and royal living quarters to the left. Surrounding the court is a honeycomb network of other sacred rooms, zigzag corridors, lustral (ceremonial washing) chambers and storerooms containing 7-foot-tall *píthoi* (clay jars).

In the **throne room,** off the central court, frescoes of griffins guard a small gypsum throne. Some suggest that this was really the ritual chair of the high priestess known as the Lady of the Labyrinth, with the sunken lustral area in front used for purification rites.

Going down the grand staircase to the left of the central court, you come to the suite of rooms Evans designated as the **royal chambers;** others now think these may have been embalming rooms. In any case, they are among the best preserved parts of the palace, intricately connected and illuminated by a remarkable device—light wells (air shafts, open above, that carried light to lower floors). Double axes incised in stone and enormous shields in a figure-eight shape mark the men's quarters; frescoes of blue dolphins, rosettes and dancing girls decorate the women's. The famous flush toilet connected to a vast drainage system is also located here. This plumbing system, built thousands of years ago by the Minoans, remains a marvel in our technological age.

Whether one accepts Evans' version of urbane Minoan elegance or other more recent theories about Knossós, the many frescoes, engraved stones and drawings on pottery show that the sacred rituals of the bull did take place here. It's not difficult to picture such an event since it is so graphically illustrated in the frescoes.

Imagine the scene around the central court 4,000 years ago. Tiers and tiers of Minoan women—their doe-eyes outlined and shadowed with green malachite, their reddened lips set off against white face paint—talk with great animation. Elaborately curled black hair, jewels and pendants dazzling in the brilliant sunlight, bare breasts and vividly coloured full-length skirts complete the picture. Minoan men lounge or stand about in their equally elaborate hair styles and jewels, their tanned bodies covered only by loincloths with tasselled cod-pieces. As elegant as the women, they are also muscular like acrobats.

White ostrich plumes held by the women brush against

The Prince of the Lilies *fresco is thought to portray a priest-king; frolicking blue dolphins grace the queen's quarters of the palace.*

the blood-red, gold-banded columns supporting the tiers. The symbolic horns of the bull decorate the tops of the buildings.

In the great courtyard there is music, and the dancers weave through familiar, ritual steps. Then men wearing leather helmets box in the blazing sun. Flowers are thrown into the ring for the victors. Acrobats cartwheel across the flower-strewn area.

Inside, in darkened chambers, the high priestess and her attendants perform their own rituals and consult a pit of sacred snakes. Elsewhere, the athletes of the main event are limbering up for their encounter with victory or death, while, in another area, enormous bulls await their turn. The doors to the sacred chambers open revealing a wide-eyed priestess holding writhing snakes. The crowd becomes quiet, listening to her utterances. Even the brilliantly arrayed king and queen in the royal box remain

Since Minoan times, the Cretans have lived off the bounteous sea and the fertile Plain of Messará.

silent. As the priestess withdraws, other doors open: the bull-leapers emerge from one, the first bull from another.

The crowd roars as the highly tuned athletes execute a succession of dazzling bull-leaping feats. Grasping the bull's horns, they vault into the air, somersault onto the animal's back and then to the ground again. Time and again, amid wild applause, they perform with flawless perfection. Until, in mid-air, one performer is impaled on the bull's horns. But it is an honourable death, one for the gods. And the games go on through the hot summer day. Other leapers are sacrificed to the bull, and then the bulls themselves are sacrificed.

By late afternoon the sports are over and the courtyard cleared. More ritual dancing follows and then feasting to honour the living and the dead. Night falls at Knossós and the celebrations continue by torchlight under the starry Cretan sky, 4,000 years ago.

Despite its ritualized cruelty, this stunning, sophisticated civilization marked a step towards the modern world. The Greeks learned much from the Minoans and, ultimately, passed this special heritage on to us.

Górtis, Phaistós and Agía Triáda

The Roman ruins of Górtis (Górtina) and the two enchanting Minoan sites of Phaistós and Agía Triáda can be combined in one excursion. If you include a swim on the south coast's Mátala beach, it makes a very full day. Tour agencies run guided tours, and public transport is available. You can call in for refreshment at the Tourist Pavilion of Phaístos, once an overnight stop for travellers. Henry Miller recorded his delightful stay here in *The Colossus of Maroussi.*

Leaving Iráklion by the Chanióporta, you follow the well-marked road to Górtis and Phaistós. About halfway along, after going through the PASS OF VOURVOULÍTI (2,000 feet above sea level), the PLAIN OF MESSARÁ opens before you. It is Crete's largest flatland and fertile area. In the distance gleams the Libyan Sea. You won't find another Knossós here. The Italians who excavated these ruins left reconstruction to the imagination of the visitor.

Scattered over a large area, **Górtis,** 45 km. from Iráklion, was already a major city about 500 B.C., when its legal code was etched on stone; it became the capital of Crete after the Romans took over in 67 B.C. but went to ruin following the Moorish invasion in the 9th century. Today you will find ancient remnants scattered over fields of flowers and amongst trees, columns and statues. The shell of the Basilica of Ágios Títos (7th century) is melodious with nesting birds, while a life-size statue of Apollo lies in the grass near his shrine. The main attraction at Górtis is the **Code of Laws,** carved on massive blocks of stone by the Dorians: 17,000 letters of archaic Doric dialect written boustrophedon style, that is, the lettering runs from right to left, left to right and so on. The laws concern both civil and criminal acts—marriage, adultery, divorce, property rights and assault.

With its superb setting, **Phaistós** (62 km. from Iráklion) is not only the most poetic Minoan site, it's also one of the most beautiful places anywhere. From the ruins, you look down the long sweep of the Messará, dotted with olive trees and vineyards, to the sea. On one side stands Mount Díkti, on the other, snow-capped Mount Ídi.

Visitors pause to admire icons in the Byzantine church in Górtis.

Caves at Mátala Beach were probably inhabited by early Christians.

The palace of Phaistós *(Festós)* was built and abandoned at the same time as Knossós, but it has no restored, blood-red columns or reconstructed frescoes. Despite the labyrinthine layout of intricate corridors and suites of rooms, Phaistós is quite different from the massive Knossós. There's a sacred feeling about the palace, so well integrated into the landscape. Without doubt, Phaistós was used by the Minoan priests and priestesses for their most holy ceremonial rites.

Like Knossós, the palace centres around a **central court** surrounded in honeycomb style by various chambers, altars and lustral basins. The walls around the court once rose to two or three storeys. Now the broken remains are overrun by wild flowers. Great flights of stairs between 40 to 65 feet wide led the Minoans up to their ceremonies. Enormous *píthoi* (clay jars) stand where they were unearthed. Inside rooms, the original, shining white gypsum walls reflect the sunlight. The alabaster paving has dramatic red bands outlining the design. A plaster wall reveals the marks of the palm and fingers of a Minoan worker.

Recent excavations show that the palace covered far more ground, probably including a Minoan village. Now farms and houses, even the Tourist Pavilion, stand over the area where Minoan structures are suspected to lie.

That most singularly haunting and mysterious of Minoan artefacts, the Phaistós Disc, was unearthed here. Everyday articles, on the other hand, were found, not at Phaistós, but at nearby Agía Triáda.

A 45-minute walk west (4 km. by car) will bring you to the royal villa of **Agía Triáda.** Since its Minoan name is unknown, the villa has come to be known by the name of the Byzantine church close by. Probably used as a hideaway by the priest-kings, Agía Triáda is a smaller version of the other Minoan palaces. Several of the greatest archaeological discoveries on Crete came from here: the *Chieftain's Cup,* the *Harvester's Vase* and the *Athlete's Vase,* now in the Iráklion museum. Agía Triáda also yielded the *Cat in a Thicket* (in Iráklion), a lovely fresco that shows with great artistic sensitivity the Minoan's interest in animals and flowers.

Though the palace has no central court or grand staircase, its rabbit warren of chambers is fascinating to wander through.

In the expanding resort of **Mátala** (about 10 km. beyond Phaistós) you can combine a swim in the Libyan Sea with a view of the famous **Mátala caves** *(Spiliés Matálon)*. Early Christians were probably the first residents of the tiers of caves, carved from the cove's wall. More recently, the Germans used them for military purposes. In the 1960s international hippies took squatter's rights. Today, the caves are a popular tourist draw.

A fine, white-sand beach slopes down to the sea, which is green and gentle here.

Beware of stones and jagged sand at nearby Agía Galíni, a booming—and often overcrowded—tourist spot. A steep, winding road leads down to the resort, situated in a narrow crevice between high cliffs.

Chic Ágios Nikólaos is a port of call for yachts and pleasure boats.

Eastern Crete

A trip on the National Highway across Crete's north coast touches on many of the island's best features. You pass by beaches and villages set between jagged mountains on one side and the Cretan Sea on the other, through landscapes of barley fields and banana plantations, carob trees and wild flowers.

Halfway between Ágios Nikólaos and Iráklion lie the neighbouring holiday towns of **Limín Chersonísou** and **Mália.** Long sandy beaches, a wide range of accommodation and proximity to some fascinating archaeological sites account for the growing popularity of both these resorts.

The **Minoan palace,** on the eastern outskirts of Mália, dates from the same era as Knossós and Phaistós. The French, who excavated Mália, did very little restoration, and you can ramble around in the evocative ruins superbly situated by the sea. Next to the ceremonial staircase you will see a remarkable **kernós,** or ceremonial table. Nearly 4 feet in diameter, 34 small depressions ring a central hollow. The table may have been part of the sacred rites with the hollows holding seeds offered to

EASTERN CRETE

ensure fertility. A ten-minute walk north-east of the palace is the *chrysólakkos* (pit of gold), a royal burial chamber, where the exquisite honeybee pendant now in the Iráklion Archaeological Museum was found.

Like all the Minoan sites, Mália has a beautiful setting. The long stretch of beach here is reputed to be the finest in Crete.

Continuing along the National Highway to Ágios Nikólaos, you can detour to the market town of NEÁPOLIS, the birthplace of Petros Philargos, Pope Alexander V. Neápolis is also known for *soumáda*, a drink made of pressed almonds that is worth trying on a hot summer day. The road descends to Ágios Nikólaos, offering magnificent views of the BAY OF MIRABÉLLO *(Kólpos Mirabéllou)* below.

Probably the most chic spot on Crete, **Ágios Nikólaos** is a small, extremely neat and pretty resort town (69 km. from Iráklion). Though a tourist mecca, crowded in mid-summer, it manages to retain much of its original harbour charm. The climate is rather dry, the winters mild and the area has been well-developed to provide the tourist with all the amenities. Ágios Nikólaos is known for its excellent sporting facilities.

Connected to the harbour by a channel is the major natural attraction of Ágios Nikólaos, the "bottomless" (200-foot-deep) LAKE VOULISMÉNI. Its landward cliff contains an aviary; along the quay-side you can take a pleasant stroll. The harbour itself, lined with *tavérnes* and souve-

Stin yiá sas—*to your health!*

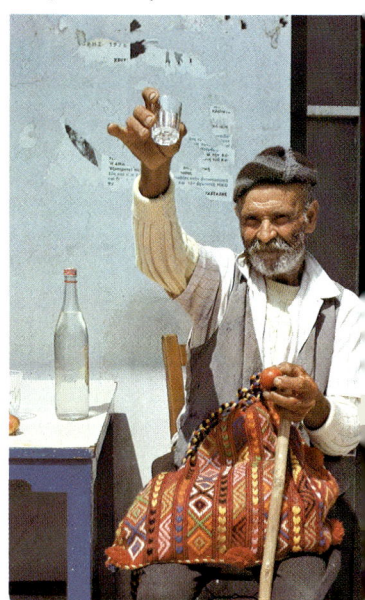

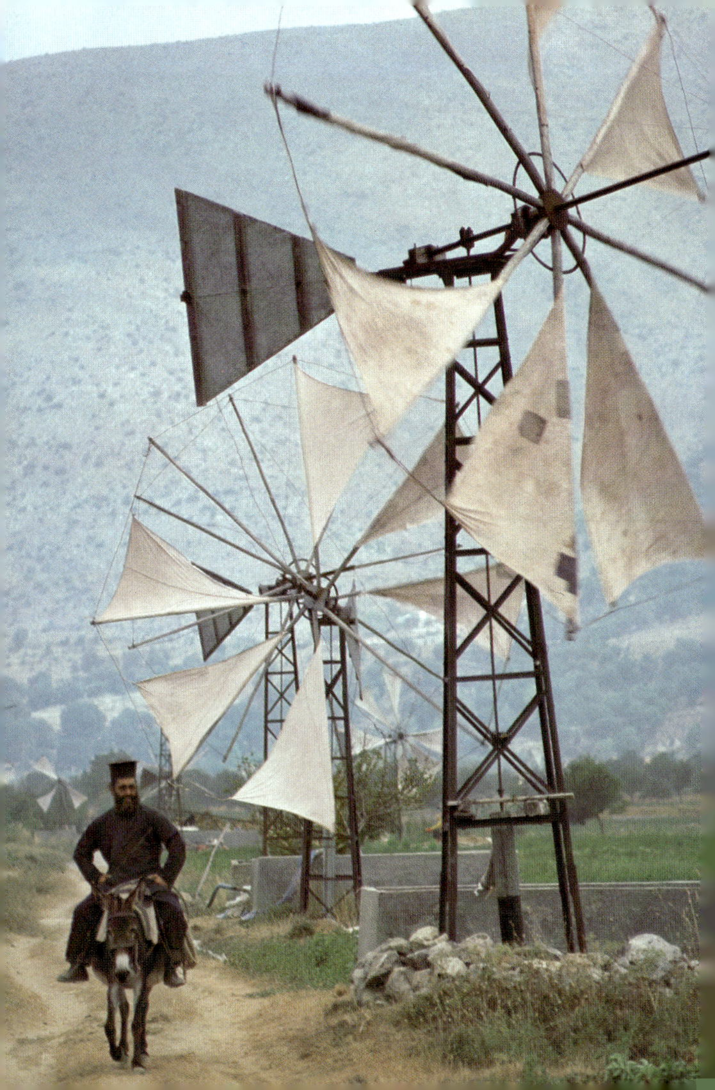

nir shops, is the place to find a wide variety of foreign tourists who have come for the sun, the sea and to meet other tourists. The town also has a good archaeological museum.

You may be too tired after daytime excursions to spend the night in one of Ágios Nikólaos' discotheques, but don't miss the evening *vólta* (promenade), followed by a leisurely dinner in one of the many good restaurants.

From Ágios Nikólaos you can make interesting excursions to the Lasíthi Plains, the village of Kritsá, the offshore island of Spinalónga (see p. 69) and the south-coast town of Ierápetra.

A trip to the LASÍTHI PLAINS *(Oropédio Lasithíou)* can be combined with a visit to the Diktaean Cave (see p. 67), said to be the birthplace of Zeus. Group tours leave from both Iráklion and Ágios Nikólaos. The mountain ride up to the pass of Lasíthi is itself a fine excursion. A huge, verdant plain opens out across the high plateau; scattered over it are the windmills of Lasíthi. Some ten thousand of them used to irrigate the plains from early summertime. Sadly, they are being replaced more and more by petrol-powered pumps.

Perched on a mountainside, KRITSÁ (12 km. from Ágios Nikólaos) commands a fine view of the Bay of Mirabéllo. The town is known for its handicrafts, especially the weaving. Several film companies have used Kritsá for locations. You'll find it an excellent background for your own picture taking.

But Kritsá's main fame comes from its 13th-century church. **Panagiá Kerá** (Most Holy Lady); its frescoes (13th and 14th century) are considered to be the finest in Crete. The small white church stands in an olive grove just outside the village. Inside, you enter a Byzantine world, peopled with angular, staring saints and visionaries.

The archaeological site of Lató will reward a 45-minute walk or a short, but rough, car ride beyond Kritsá. This Doric and later Hellenistic town, locally known as GOULÁS, is more notable for its stunning setting than for its archaeological interest. The view down through olive groves and almond trees to the sea far below can safely be qualified as breathtaking.

GOURNIÁ (18 km. from

Cloth-sailed windmills still to be found watering Lasíthi Plains.

Whitewashed houses reflect the strong sunlight, cooling the interiors. Right: icon in Toploú Monastery.

Ágios Nikólaos) merits a stop. The most completely preserved Minoan town, it was excavated by Harriet Boyd-Hawes, an American archaeologist. Visitors are usually surprised to see how much Gourniá, last inhabited over 3,000 years ago, resembles a contemporary Cretan village.

Crossing Crete at its narrowest point, you come to IERÁPETRA (38 km. from Ágios Nikólaos), the only large town on the south coast. The elegant and practical scythe-shaped knives you see in souvenir shops all over Crete are produced here. Because of its mild climate Ierápetra is expanding rapidly as a tourist centre, even in the winter months. Its assets include a good beach, a museum and the remains of a Venetian fort on the quay, a Turkish mosque and minaret in town and a seafront lined with *tavérnes* and discotheques. Ierápetra retains a distinctly Oriental flavour.

From Ágios Nikólaos to the town of Sitía on the east, you travel along a superb coast known as the Riviera of Crete. The corniche winds past white villages set on steep slopes, with orchards and olive groves on one side and a sharp drop to the sea on the other. The ride is not for the faint-hearted. The town of SITÍA (73 km. from Ágios Nikólaos) is a quaint harbour town. The Venetians had hoped to make it a major city—and there are still a few Venetian ruins about—but earthquakes, its isolated location, and the Turkish pirate Barbarossa (see p. 20) spoiled their plans. Museums and a restored fort make Sitía worth visiting, as do the beaches, restaurants and summer raisin festival. The town is port-of-call for boats travelling between Rhodes and Santoríni and has flights to Rhodes as well as Kássos and Kárpathos.

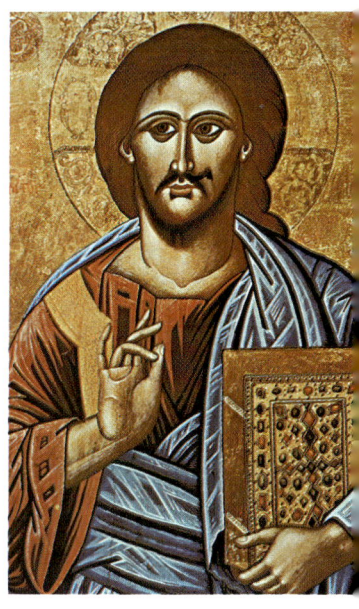

At the very eastern end of Crete is the fourth main Minoan palace site, **Káto Zákros** (115 km. from Ágios Nikólaos). The road—no longer the National Highway—travels across a high plateau with a view of a vast gorge, and then winds down towards the sea amid banana plantations. Though smaller than Knossós, the palace of Káto Zákros follows the same basic plan. Surrounding the palace are extensive remains of a Minoan town. The archaeological finds include many pieces of fine workmanship, among them a rhyton (animal-shaped vessel) carved from rock crystal, now in the Archaeological Museum of Iráklion. These show that remote Káto Zákros also shared in the glories of the Minoan civilization. Since thorough excavations only began in 1962, new treasures may still be unearthed here. After a look at the ruins, you may just feel like loafing on the beach or in a local *tavérna*.

Halfway between Sitía and Káto Zákros, a turn-off and a short, rough road leads to the **Monastery of Toploú** (from the Turkish word for "cannon", because of the large cannon used for defence). Standing in splendid isolation, the much-restored 14th-century monastery contains the "Lord, Thou Art Great" **icon** by Ioánnis Kornáros (1770), considered to be a masterpiece of Cretan art.

The beach of Váï lies on the north-eastern tip of Crete. After dusty mountain drives and strenuous excursions into ancient history, you might appreciate cooling off in the sea at this fine, sandy beach. Váï, which means "palm" in Greek, is in fact ringed with palm trees, said to have come from date stones dropped here by the Arab invaders. Since it is not an undiscovered beach, you may find it crowded.

Váï, the palm beach of Crete—a favourite spot since Classical times.

Western Crete

The broad National Highway goes west from Iráklion to Réthimnon and Chaniá. Just out of Iráklion it passes close to Fódele, the village where the painter El Greco was reputedly born. Though the Highway is not as spectacular as the eastern segment, it passes through some very pretty scenery. Surrounded by yellow broom, scarlet poppies and green orchards, and lined with miles of beaches, the road runs along the Cretan Sea in view of the mountains. In recent years, resort hotels have sprung up all along the coast, dramatically changing the atmosphere of this once-tranquil area of the island.

An alternate route takes you from Phaistós to Réthimnon via the south coast. This trip, passing through rich farm lands and over a mountain range, provides a view of Cretan life off the main tourist routes. Though only about 80 kilometres long, the road is anything but straight, so allow yourself enough time to visit some of the interesting villages along the way.

Inland is Spíli with its cascading fountains. A short detour from the main route takes you down through a gorge to the Monastery of Préveli. Built near the sea, the monastery served as a refuge for the Cretan resistance during both the Turkish and the German occupations. Geórgios Psychoundákis, a resistance fighter, tells of his experiences under the Germans in *The Cretan Runner*.

The remainder of the trip to Réthimnon runs through countryside that resembles the semi-arid landscape of the south of France.

Many tourists consider that **Réthimnon** (78 km. from Iráklion) is still one of the most charming spots in Greece. Though the third largest city in Crete (pop. 20,000), Réthimnon is calm and well maintained. It spreads out around a curve of bay with a sweeping stretch of beach. Other pleasant beaches extend to either side of Réthimnon, its modern harbour and old Venetian port.

The narrow, meandering streets leading from the sea give the town the feeling of a North African *medina*. Many of the streets are too narrow for traffic. Architectural mixtures of Venetian and Turkish styles predominate, with the rounded stone arches of the Venetians topped by the wooden overhanging balco-

WESTERN CRETE

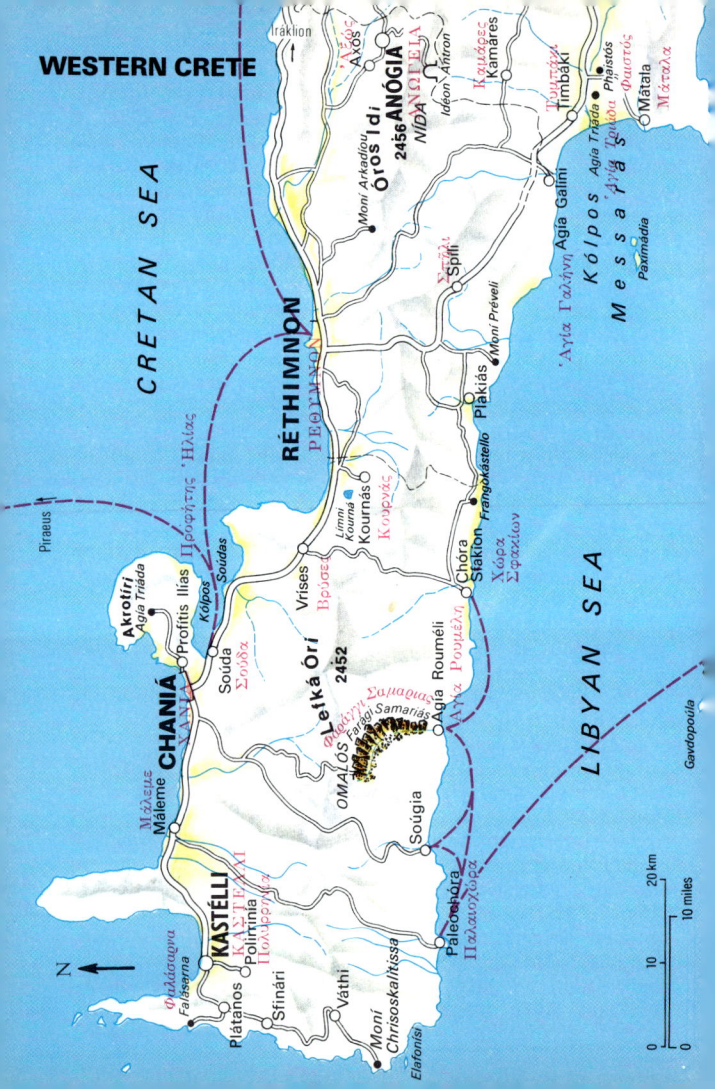

nies of the Turks. Edward Lear—better known for his nonsense verse—painted a series of watercolours here. These show that the town has hardly changed in more than a hundred years.

Overlooking the city is the huge Venetian **Fortétza.** To get there you climb a series of ancient steps from Odós Melissinoú. Little remains of the fort except for the imposing outer walls which command a panoramic view of the sea. Within the walls stand various pieces of ruined arches and arcades and the shell of a mosque guarded by a single palm tree.

The public gardens in the centre of Réthimnon are a popular meeting place. In the midst of exotic trees and flowers and a small zoo, the Cretan Wine Festival takes place here in late July. Réthimnon has a number of minarets that were attached to Venetian churches by the Turks. From the balconies of the **Mosque of Neranziés** *(Djamí ton Neranzión),* where the faithful were once called to prayer, you have a fine view of the city. Nearby, the lion-headed Arimondi Fountain—a hotchpotch of Venetian and Turkish stone work which defies perspective—continues to

Réthimnon's lazy harbour is framed by picturesque Venetian houses.

function. Across the intersections is an elegant, stone-arched, 17th-century Venetian loggia that housed a small archaeological museum (now in a former prison building near the Fortétza). Continue to the seafront promenade. Lined with outdoor cafés, restaurants, souvenir shops and newspaper stands, this is where Réthimnon takes its evening *vólta*.

The **Monastery of Arkádi** is only a 45-minute ride away. Buses leave Réthimnon from Platía Moátsou. As so often in Crete, the short distance can take you from a quiet beach to a craggy mountainside. The road runs along a spectacular gorge up to the monastery. Arkádi is both beautifully situated and famous. Besieged by Turkish troops in 1866, the abbot of this resistance and refugee centre ordered the explosion of the gunpowder magazine rather than surrender. His decision caused the death of nearly 1,000 Cretans inside Arkádi and as many Turks outside, forever symbolizing the Cretan slogan of "Freedom or death". Now somewhat restored, the 16th-century façade of the monastery provides a good example of ornate Venetian. The Cretans celebrate the explosion date, November 9, as their national holiday, gathering for memorial services in Réthimnon and Arkádi. But never solemn for long, the islanders follow the ceremonies with fireworks and, inevitably, music and dancing.

The one-hour drive on the National Highway from Réthimnon to Chaniá doesn't have to be hot and dusty. You can stop off along the way to swim at any of the many beaches lining the road. You also pass near KOURNÁ, the only freshwater lake on Crete. Just before Soúda Bay, there's a massive Venetian fortress, called Izzedine after the Turks took it over.

If you come into Chaniá on the overnight ferry from Piraeus, you enter by the spectacular land-locked harbour of SOÚDA BAY *(Kólpos Soúdas)*. The cafés in the town's little square are filled with sailors, since the harbour serves as a naval base for both the Greeks and for NATO. The long, green slope at the head of the bay is a military cemetery for the British and Commonwealth soldiers who died defending Crete during World War II.

An agreeable mixture of Venetian and Turkish influences, **Chaniá** (150 km. from

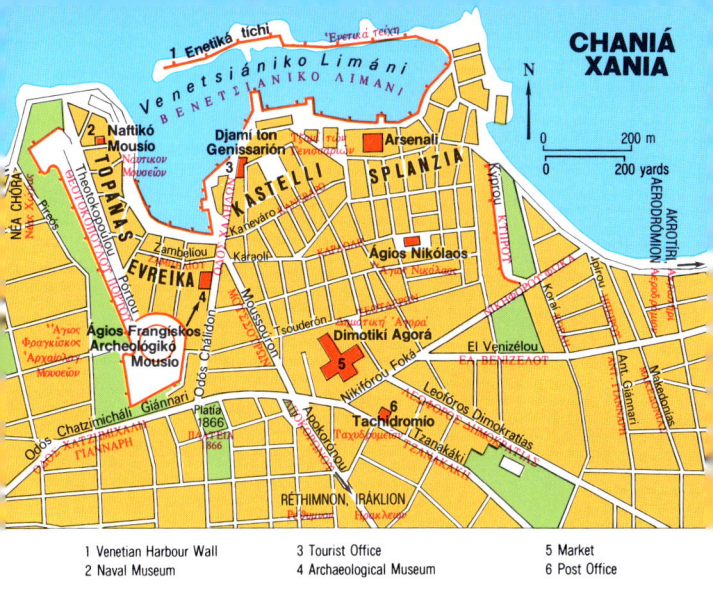

1 Venetian Harbour Wall
2 Naval Museum
3 Tourist Office
4 Archaeological Museum
5 Market
6 Post Office

Iráklion) is renowned for its hospitality. A covered **market**, modelled after the one in Marseilles, dominates the centre of the town. The stalls overflow with Cretan produce—fruits, vegetables, flowers, cheese, meat and fish. This is the place to buy dittany, the rare herb gathered from mountainsides, which the Cretans use to make a curative tea. Across Odós Chatzimicháli and beyond the post office are the public gardens, a cool place to escape the summer sun or linger in an outdoor café. Children like the zoo and aviary here. At the top of Odós Chálidon, you will find a square, Platía 1866, planted with palms and orange trees. Enjoy the splendid view of the White Mountains *(Lefká Óri),* snow-capped well into late spring.

Going down Chálidon towards the old harbour, turn to the right into Odós Skridlof, the place to look for leather goods of all kinds, including hand-made shoes and boots. **57**

In the shops lining Chálidon, merchants offer a bumper crop of Cretan souvenirs. The Church of Ágios Frangískos on your left, a typical example of Venetian building on Crete, now contains an archaeological museum. You might pass without noticing (the door in the recess on the right on entering is often closed) the charming enclosed courtyard complete with Venetian doorways and a Turkish fountain.

You'll probably spend most of your time in Chaniá—when you're not on the beach—around the **harbour**. The western loop of the harbour bay is lined with restaurants, cafés and tourist shops selling Cretan handicrafts. At one end stands the **Mosque of the Janissaries** (1645), now a tourist information centre, facing —across the water—the **Firkás**, a restored part of the original Venetian wall. Housed here, appropriately enough, is the Naval Museum. Sections of the immense inner wall that surrounded the city are scattered all over Chaniá, often where you least expect to see a wall.

Walking eastwards along the quay from the tourist office, you will come to the *arsenali,* dating from the time when the Venetians hoped to make Chaniá the "Venice of the East". From the long breakwater of golden stone, which ends in a Turkish lighthouse, you have a superb view of the harbour and the town.

After a day on the beach, almost everyone heads for the harbour, *the* place to promenade in the evening when it's closed to traffic. Enjoy a late dinner here, with the rest of Chaniá, while the waves lap the quay near your table. Then take your after-dinner coffee at one of the tables with sun shades near the mosque, in view of the lighthouse and the open sea beyond.

The area behind the harbour, the **Kastélli quarter** (or *synikía*), is an intriguing jumble of historical and modern Crete. Excavations here have uncovered the ancient town of Kydonía, one of the three main cities of Crete in the post-Minoan era. Chaniá was built right on top of it. The excavations tend to move site according to local building requirements, but you may be lucky enough to see traces of the settlement on sites along Odós Kaneváro behind the mosque. The quarter's Venetian palace and mansions were largely destroyed in the bombings during World War II.

The Church of **Ágios Nikólaos** (St. Nicholas) nestles in the midst of intimate winding streets in the Splánzia quarter. Erected by the Venetians, the church has a graceful Turkish minaret balanced by a Greek Orthodox bell tower. Another lovely minaret stands nearby.

Synikía Topanás, the old Turkish section, occupies the

One of Chaniá's intriguing back alleys; below: the way to see the town in fitting style and comfort.

Boots are bargains on an island where craftsmen still flourish.

narrow lanes behind the Firkás. Here you will find Venetian stone houses topped by wooden upper storeys added on by the Turks. At the corner of Odós Zambelíou and Móschon stands the Renieri Gate (1608). Wedged between houses and a restaurant, it's difficult to get a good overall view of it.

The **Evréïka quarter** (from Odós Zambelíou to the harbour) was the Jewish section of Chaniá.

When you're ready to swim, the city has a swimming pool just beyond the Firkás. Ten minutes further on you come to Néa Chóra, a public beach with outdoor *travérnes* under shade trees. If this is too crowded, continue walking along the sea until you find a sandy stretch that suits your mood. Most beaches outside the city limits and not connected to resorts offer little in the way of amenities, but you're more likely to have a patch of sand to yourself here.

Excursions from Chaniá to AKROTÍRI (meaning promontory) include two Cretan landmarks. **Profitis Ilías** was the scene of an illustrious chapter in the island's history. Here in 1897, during a brief struggle involving the four great powers and the Turks, Cretan insurgents defiantly raised the flag of Greece to show their solidarity with the mainland. The flag was shot away. But, according to the story, when one courageous Cretan stood up with the standard in his hand, the guns fell silent. The tomb of statesman Eleftherios Venizélos lies nearby.

The Monastery of **Agía Triáda** (17 km. from Chaniá) is set in surprisingly gentle countryside for Crete. As you approach by a long avenue of trees, the monumental 17th-century façade comes into view. Formerly a seminary, this is one of the major monasteries in Crete; visitors are always welcome to wander around the grounds and visit the church.

You can walk (a one-hour hike) or drive through a herb- and flower-strewn landscape to an isolated monastery, Moní Gouvernétou. More ambitious tourists might consider continuing on (another hour) to the abandoned Monastery of Katholikó and the caves of Early Christian hermits. One of these has particularly stunning stalagmites.

Several spectacular day trips, involving crossing the island's backbone, are possible from Chaniá. The first, to the south coast and the village of Chóra Sfakíon (74 km.), can be made by bus or car. You pass through VOUNÁ SFAKÍON, a craggy mountain range inhabited by the legendary Sfakiotes whose struggles over the centuries kept them free from Venetian, Turkish and German occupations. In spite of the recent intrusion by the outside world, you can still catch a glimpse of a vanishing outpost of individuality in these villages. And don't worry about your reception—the Sfakiotes' hospitality to visitors is as lavish as their proud and fierce reputation. After a drive through the rugged mountains, you come to CHÓRA SFAKÍON, a quiet village with a beach. Thousands of troops were evacuated from the island here following the Battle of Crete in 1941.

Twelve kilometres to the east of Chóra Sfakíon lies the Venetian fort of **Frangokástello**. An awesome sight, the remains of the grandiose fort overlook the sea. Four corner towers and the inevitable Lion of St. Mark are left. For some mysterious reason—possibly weather conditions—an eerie mist surrounds the castle at dawn in mid-May, creating a mirage in which Cretans claim to see the ghosts of Sfakiotes who died defending the fort against the Turks.

From Chaniá, there's also a bus service to SOÚGIA on the south coast (70 km.) and the archaeological site of LISSÓS.

Travelling to the west of Crete from Chaniá will take you into relatively undeveloped country. The road passes through the resort complex of MÁLEME, principal site of the Battle of Crete in May 1941. The main town on western Crete, KASTÉLLI KISSÁMOU (42 km. from Chaniá), is located on a splendid gulf with some of the finest, unbroken stretches of sandy beach on the island. The 8th-century B.C. ruins of POLYRRINÍA nearby are better known for the magnificent view than for the archaeological interest of the site. Beyond the crest of the western tip lies the long curving beach of FALÁSARNA. A bus from Kastélli serves the tiny village of **Sfinári**—a real escapist's paradise. But be prepared to spend the night. The return service doesn't depart until the following day.

From Chaniá, a two-hour bus journey will take you to the isolated nunnery of CHRISOSKALÍTISSA. To get there, you pass through a number of picturesque villages, where a different world opens up. But be careful—the only accommodation is in the village of VÁTHI, and it is very limited.

The tiny island of GÁVDOS off the south coast is a bare, sparsely populated place believed to be the nymph Calypso's island in *The Odyssey*. Visited by boat from the village of CHÓRA SFAKÍON or PALEOCHÓRA, Gávdos is one of those places where you take away what you bring to it. But, at least you can say you've been there.

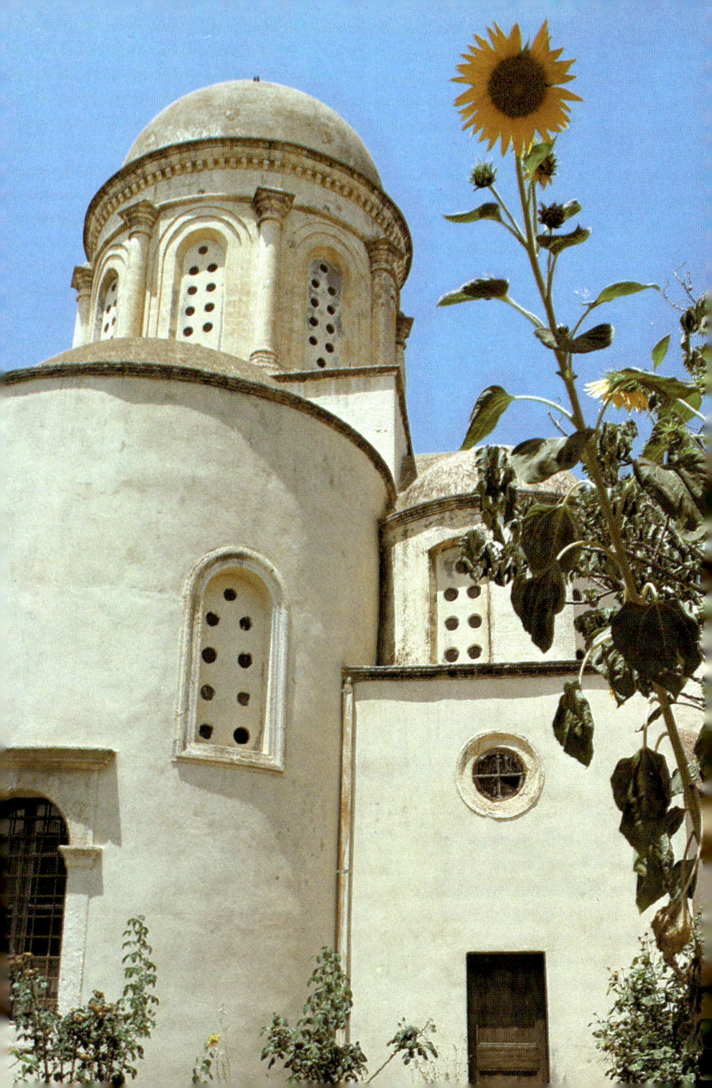

Excursions

Gorge of Samariá
(Farági Samariás)

One of the most extraordinary adventures of Crete is a visit to the Gorge of Samariá. Reputed to be the longest gorge in Europe, walking through it may take anywhere from four to seven hours. Count on a full day for the outing, including the drive from and back to Chaniá.

The gorge—a National Park—is open from 6 a.m. to 3 p.m., and only between May 1 and October 31 because the winter rains make it impassable. Tour agencies will offer excursions with guides and transport, and regular buses from Chaniá take you directly to the plain of OMALÓS (42 km.) where the walk begins. Just bring along a sensible pair of shoes, a hat and a water bottle.

For most tourists, walking the gorge poses no undue difficulties, though the terrain is rough and rocky and the heat can be enervating. If you think you might not make it on foot, donkeys are available for hire —at a price.

From the town of Omalós, you take the *xylóskalon* ("wooden steps", in actual fact a zigzag path), 2,500 feet down into the gorge itself. Ahead of you are 11 miles of spectacular scenery.

After a two- to three-hour walk, the path goes by the stone huts of the now-deserted village of Samariá, named after the Venetian Church of Santa Maria here. While the sun shines on the world above, parts of the gorge are immersed in evocative shadows and mists. No wonder Cretan legends peopled the place with gods and goddesses. The gorge was used as a refuge during the years of occupation and war. Today its only inhabitant is the wild Cretan ibex, the *agrími*. If you're lucky you may see one leaping across the higher ledges—a sport recommended only for *agrími*. Dittany, a herb much prized by Cretans, grows here. It's always been associated with the domain of the *agrími*, for both are difficult to find.

Thousands of years of winter torrents have carved fantastic shapes into the walls of the gorge. Rock formations resembling Gothic cathedrals swirl up the walls or turn into castle-like battlements. You can distinguish millenniums of the earth's strata in the varicoloured layers. In summer, the river dries to a trickle, turning up here and there or forming ice-cold reflecting pools. For the remainder of the walk, you follow the dry river bed or a higher path under the towering walls. Pine and cypress grow here as do fig trees, bursting with fruit. Thyme and all kinds of wild flowers emerge from crevices, scenting the cool air.

A hike to do in summer; winter rains make the gorge impassable.

In the narrow pass of *sideróportes* (iron gates) the walls of the gorge, only yards wide, rise to a height of 1,000 feet, blocking out the sun. The pass brings you to the village of AGÍA ROUMÉLI with its masses of oleanders. Though the entry to the gorge involved a steep descent, you leave by a great gash in the rock walls opening out onto an alluvial plain along the Libyan Sea.

Agía Rouméli is the site of the ancient city of Tárra (5th century B.C. to 5th century A.D.). The Venetians built a church right on top of the ruins of a **temple of Apollo.** You can see the temple's black, white and red mosaic floor in the forecourt of the church of the Panagía. A large stone found here in 1937 bears the relief of a hand grasping the sacred double axe of the Minoans—evidence that the Minoans penetrated even the remotest parts of Crete.

At the end of the gorge, you can either stay overnight in Agía Rouméli or take a regularly scheduled boat to

Chóra Sfakíon to the east or westwards to Soúgia and/or Paleochóra. The one-hour trip to Chóra Sfakíon offers a magnificent view of the craggy southern coast.

It's a good idea to arrive at the docks well ahead of time, as these services are often overbooked. When a boat is full it may just depart—ahead of schedule.

Caves and Mountain Climbing

The two most famous caves on Crete, on Mount Díkti and Mount Ídi, are both associated with the god Zeus.

The **Diktaean Cave** *(Diktéon Ántron)*, purported to be the birthplace of Zeus, can be combined with a visit to the Lasíthi Plains. The easiest way to visit the cave is on an organized tour from Iráklion or Ágios Nikólaos. Bring a good torch as the cave is inadequately lit. And equip yourself with proper footwear, for the entrance to the cave— some 5 kilometres beyond the village of Psichró—is steep and slightly tricky and the cave damp and slippery.

Agía Rouméli Church, built on top of Roman mosaics; right: a visit to one of Crete's legendary caves.

Discovered by the Cretans in the 1880s, and excavated in 1899 by D. G. Hogarth, the cave contained artefacts which indicate that the Minoans used it as a shrine. With its stalagmites and stalactites of over 200 feet, the interior is quite spectacular. There's a admission fee.

According to legend, the great god Kronos had been warned he would be overthrown by a son. His wife, Rhea, hit Zeus in the Diktaean Cave when he was born, raising him in the Idaian Cave.

The climb to the summit of the mountain starts in the village of ÁGIOS GEÓRGIOS (4 km. before Psichró).

Though hardly an alpine peak, this mountain (7,045 feet) is not for the casual tourist and should not be attempted without a guide. Those who make the six-hour climb will be rewarded with a superb view of the entire island of Crete.

Mount Ídi, more commonly known as Psilorítis, is an even more arduous adventure. It is advisable to engage a

At least donkeys don't run out of fuel; right: seaside fun for all.

guide—check with the Tourist Organization in Iráklion or Réthymnon before attempting this hike.

Two routes lead to the cave and the summit. The easiest way to get there from Iráklion, is through the village of Anógia (35 km., see p. 70). After you climb to the top, you can come down the other side of the mountain to the village of KAMÁRES then take a bus to Iráklion.

Doing the hike in reverse, you begin in Kamáres, where you spend the night. Then, starting out at dawn, you can visit the cave of Kamáres on the way up, an easy four-hour climb. The lovely Minoan pottery known as Kamáres ware (now in the Iráklion museum) was found here. Six more hours should bring you to the top of Mount Ídi, the highest point in Crete (8,058 feet), covered with snow almost year-round. Despite the difficulties, a surprising number of travellers do make this climb. The **Idaian Cave** *(Idéon Antron)* lies four or five hours down towards the PLAIN OF NÍDA *(Pediáda tis Nídas)*.

Discovered by some Italian explorers, the cave contained 9th- and 8th-century B.C. bronze shields (also in the Iráklion museum).

Overnight accommodation for the hardy usually consists of either a tent en route or the Chapel of the Crucifix, at the top of Mount Ídi.

You continue along the Nidhan Plain to Anógia, where you can get a bus to Iráklion.

Islands

Far easier than traversing a gorge or climbing a mountain is a boat trip to a nearby island (for the excursion to Gávdos, see page 62). SPINALÓNGA can be reached from ELOÚNDA (12 km. north of Ágios Nikólaos) or by boat from Ágios Nikólaos, an excursion offered by several agencies.

The island of Spinalónga contains a Venetian fort, built in 1579, that is impressive because of its imposing location. The Turks took over the fort in 1715, and it later became a leper colony (but there's no danger of contracting leprosy here).

On the nearby peninsula, also called Spinalónga, is ancient OLOÚS. A mosaic floor depicting dolphins can be seen in the ruins of an Early Christian church. The old port and possibly parts of the old city, now submerged, could be of interest to skin-divers.

The tiny islands of PSÍRA and MÓCHLOS, across the Bay of Mirabéllo from Ágios Nikólaos, can also be visited on boat excursions. Each contains ruins of Minoan settlements.

In summer, boats ply the route from Ierápetra to the quiet little island of CHRISÍ (Gaidouronísi). Swim, have a meal at the *tavérna* and enjoy the peace and tranquillity.

Just off the south-west coast, the idyllic ELAFONÍSI ISLANDS lie within wading distance of the mainland. You can cross from Paleochóra or with a tour that starts in Chaniá. Some glorious beaches await you, but don't count on spending the night. Hotels have yet to be built on the islands.

Cretan Village Outing

Local travel agencies feature excursions to two typical villages in central Crete. Though you'll hardly be among the first group of tourists to venture into town, your visit can be interesting and a good deal of fun.

The people of ANÓGIA near

Mount Ídi put on a rousing display of traditional dances. You'll have the opportunity to sample some of the pleasant local wines and do some shopping.

Just as popular is an evening and on-into-the-night party in KARZÁNOS, near Ágios Nikólaos. Here you'll be offered a hearty Cretan dinner with wine.

Winnowing wheat—the natural way—on the fertile Plains of Lasíthi.

Bouzoúki and lýra music sets the rhythm for dancers on Crete.

What to Do

Music and Dance

Music is definitely the pulse beat of Crete. You'll hear it throbbing everywhere—coming from radios, *tavérnes* or people singing in the street.

Through films, the music of composers like Míkis Theodorákis and Mános Hadjidákis has become familiar all over the world. The two kinds of Greek music you'll hear most often on Crete—frequently accompanied by dancing—are *bouzoúki* and *lýra*.

Named after the mandoline-like instrument, *bouzoúki* is enjoying a strong revival in Greece. It originated in the slums and opium dens of 19th-century Piraeus. The music and the lyrics, always played very loud, are direct; the driving rhythms hypnotic.

The men dance in an open space in front of the band—alone, in pairs or in a group. Women, traditionally, perform in the village squares. Often the movements make it seem more like an athletic event. But when you see a Cretan dancing alone, he's expressing his mood of the moment, whether of great happiness or sorrow.

The *lýra* is an instrument similar to a violin, which is held on the knee and bowed. It produces the exotic, whining sound usually identified with Middle Eastern music.

The many traditional dances of Crete have come down through the generations. They include the *chaniótikos,* a circle dance; the *pendozáli,* arms interlocked in an animated dance; and the *syrtós,* a stately circle dance. On any occasion—whether a wedding, a festival or just a get-together—you'll find music and dancing.

The traditional costumes are often seen at celebrations and always at the festivals. The women usually wear long skirts covered by beautifully hand-embroidered white aprons, as well as peasant blouses, also thickly embroidered. Light veils and jewellery, usually necklaces of small gold coins and beads that have been in the family for years, complete the costume. The men wear baggy, knee-length black or royal blue pants, black shirt and embroidered waistcoat. In their cummerbunds they carry their traditional knives. Around their heads, tassel-fringed black cloth, on their feet, white boots.

Besides the *tavérnes* and the impromptu village celebrations, you will certainly find traditional music and dancing at Chaniá's "Battle of Crete" folklore festival in May and the Cretan Wine Festival in Réthimnon in July, as well as at many of the religious and agricultural festivals on the island (see p. 74). Visitors are always welcome. But, be warned: Cretan hospitality knows no bounds, and this is especially true at their celebra-

Principal Festivals

January 6	Epiphany *(ton Theofaníon)*. This is the day when the waters are blessed throughout Greece. A bishop throws a cross into the water, and the young men dive for it. The one who retrieves the cross is honoured.
Carnival *(Apókries)*	The two weeks preceding Lent are given over to costume parties and general high spirits. Iráklion and Réthimnon have the most colourful celebrations.
Clean Monday	*Katharí Deftéra,* the start of Orthodox Lent and a day of fasting. The Cretan skies are filled with kites because it's traditionally a day of kite flying.
Orthodox Good Friday and Easter	*Megáli Paraskeví, Páscha.* Candlelight funeral processions with a flower-bedecked bier pass through the streets at night. Midnight services on Holy Saturday announce *Christós Anésti* (Christ is risen). The paschal candle is lit, church bells peal and fireworks light up the sky. General feasting follows.
second half of May	Folklore festival in Chaniá marking the anniversary of the Battle of Crete.
June 24	St. Johns the Baptist *(tou Agíou Ioánnou)*. Bonfires are lit all over Greece. The custom is to jump over the fire, though generally only young boys do it.
second half of July	Cretan Wine Festival in Réthimnon, including wine sampling, music and dancing.
August 15	Assumption Day *(tis Panagías)*. The village of Móchlos, near Iráklion, has a festival with dancing, fireworks and exhibitions of local crafts. Neápolis celebrates on August 14 and 15.
August 31	Holy Sash of the Virgin *(tis Agías Zónis)*. A great festival in the village of Psichró on the Plains of Lasíthi with local dances and feasting.
November 7-9	Anniversary of 1866 Explosion (see p. 56). Crete's own "national holiday", it's celebrated with proper enthusiasm. The Monastery of Arkádi and the city of Réthimnon hold festivities and much dancing.

tions. You may find that once you're there, with the food, local wines and all that music and dancing, you won't be able to leave easily.

Films

All foreign films are shown in their original language with Greek subtitles. Many outdoor cinemas operate in summer. The doors open at 7 p.m., but the film does not begin until after dark. Also be prepared for at least one official break—not to mention the unofficial breaks or breakdowns—so that the pistachio seller can wander up and down the aisles.

Museums and Archaeological Sites

An admission fee is charged to visit the museums and archaeological sites. On weekdays, the sites open at 8 or 10 a.m. Most close at 7 p.m., some at 6 or 5 or even 4 p.m. On Sundays and holidays they open at 9 a.m. and close between 1 and 6 p.m. Check with your hotel receptionist or the tourist office before visiting.

The Archaeological Museum, Iráklion, houses the most important collection of Minoan art and artefacts in the world (see p. 30).

Fabrics are always a good buy on Crete with wide selection even at the smallest handicraft shops.

The museum is open from 8 a.m. to 7 p.m., Tuesday to Sunday, and from 12.30 to 7 p.m. on Mondays.

The Historical Museum, Iráklion, covers the island's history from Byzantine to modern times (see p. 32). Open 9 a.m. to 5 p.m. Monday to Friday and 9 a.m. to 2 p.m. on Saturdays (closed Sundays).

You will also find small archaeological museums in Chaniá, Réthimnon and Ágios Nikólaos (closed Tuesdays).

The smaller museums and various churches close for a midday break. On Greek Christmas, New Year and Easter, March 25 and October 28, all museums are closed.

Shopping

Generally, hours are 8.30 a.m. to 1.30 p.m. and 5.30 to 8.30 p.m. Tuesdays, Thursdays and Fridays and 8.30 a.m. to 2 p.m. Mondays, Wednesdays and Saturdays. But a shop might be open late or shut on Saturday. On the 'wrong' afternoon, a newsstand can often help with minor necessities like stamps, cigarettes or aspirins.

Best Buys
Crete is small enough so that most of its products circulate freely and will show up in tourist shops everywhere. A government-sponsored display in Réthimnon (in the Tourist Information Centre building on the seafront) gathers together all the handcrafted and manufactured items of Crete. It's helpful to look over their selection, but only wholesale dealers can buy there.

Crete is well known for its

beautiful fabrics. Formerly, the wool was carded and spun by hand. Every Cretan village still has several looms for turning the goods into cloth.

The grade of material runs from very fine to the coarsest goat-hair type. It's made into an enormous range of articles: clothing for both men and women, bedspreads and pillow covers, curtains and those brightly coloured Greek shoulder bags, *tagária* (known on Crete as the *voúrgia*). If you want to buy the material by the bolt, most shops will ship it for you—a colourful reminder of your stay, even though prices aren't as low as they once were.

Another excellent buy is hand-knitted sweaters. The basic, white seamen's sweater, always associated with Greece, has a distinctive square neck and short sleeves. Make sure the wool isn't too coarse or you'll feel it through whatever you wear.

In many villages, wool was carded and spun by hand; selling fresh produce the old-fashioned way.

Countless ladies in black sit in front of their white-washed houses on Crete making endless bands of lace. In many villages you can buy directly from these women, and the price is sure to be far lower than in the shops.

Boot-making has been raised almost to an art in Crete. Particularly in the west, you'll find bootmakers who do all the work by hand—and made to measure. Handmade shoes, on the other hand, tend to be sturdy rather than fashionable.

Woodcarvers, like bootmakers, often cluster together in a city. The tourist can wander from one shop to another, comparing the work and watching this ancient craft. Wood carving on Crete includes small items like handmade letter openers as well as furniture. Chairs with sculpted backs and legs are especially recommended.

Iráklion has many pottery factories, and others are scattered along the north coast. You can buy from shops or go directly to the factories. If you're concerned about breakage, consider buying an alabaster ashtray or bowl. On the other hand, alabaster souvenirs weigh much more than fragile pottery.

Antiques

The antiques you can still find on Crete are more likely "old" than "antique". Stay clear of any "Minoan" or "Roman" artefacts. Even if they do prove to be genuine, the complicated Greek laws and the paperwork required should be enough to discourage you.

The best old buys are carpets, bedspreads with lace flounces and embroidered cloths—all faded with time but quite lovely. Much of this comes from unclaimed dowries. You won't find these old materials in the usual tourist souvenir shops, so ask around. And shop around. Prices and quality vary enormously.

Souvenirs

Phaistós Disc paperweights and painted plastic Minoan goddesses abound in the tourist shops. Better souvenirs include the handmade knives from the town of Ierápetra, often with an inscription in Greek on the blade, and worry beads *(kombolóïa)*.

Replicas of Minoan jewellery—in particular the "honey-bee pendant" seen in the Iráklion Archaeological Museum—can be very attractive. But shop around until you find the best. Reproductions of icons make inexpensive souvenirs.

Where to Shop

Shops selling tourist items line the main streets and squares of most of the towns and villages. The largest city, Iráklion, also has the greatest selection, but you may find more charming things elsewhere. The villages of Kritsá and Anógia in central Crete are noted for their fine handicrafts, and buying directly from the artisan can involve some savings. Anógia in particular is famed for its lace and wool. A tour round the weaving factory is an unusual and well worthwhile experience—in addition to the splendid drive or bus ride into the mountains.

By all means, wander off the main tourist street in any town. You'll find the atmosphere less frantic, the service less commercial and perhaps a different choice of goods. Some of the least usual items are to be found in the markets—Iráklion and Chaniá especially, where bundles of dried herbs hang next to the aluminium *bríki*—the special little coffee pot you need to make Greek coffee at home.

Bargaining

Though the prices of most items—food, hotel accommodation, even souvenirs—are clearly marked and government regulated, old carpets, woven goods and the like are worth bargaining over. If you think you've a talent for it, plunge in. But don't forget, the shopkeeper has more experience at this game. Still, if you both play fair—and all's fair in haggling—you could find yourself with a bargain.

Sports and Outdoor Activities

With its magnificent beaches, the major outdoor activity on Crete is naturally swimming —or just lying on the beach perfecting a Mediterranean tan. The more active tourists do a bit of water-skiing or dive into the clear waters with masks and fins.

Pale-skinned northerners should take their first days of strong Cretan sun with moderation. Even in winter, the rays may surprise you with a bad burn if you're not careful. An old Cretan sunburn remedy is yoghurt. Though its efficacy has never been scientifically proven, it's very cooling.

Boating, Water-skiing and Windsurfing

Crete has many harbours, but few of them are set up for renting small craft or sailing boats. Would-be mariners must also cope with the island's unpredictable winds. Welcome as they are in the summer heat, they make sailing a somewhat exasperating and hazardous adventure.

Ágios Nikólaos, Eloúnda Beach and Mínos Beach, around the protected Bay of Mirabéllo, have the best facilities for boating and other water sports, down to canoes and pedal-boats. Another natural playground for the adventurous is Réthimnon, which offers para-gliding and, not far from town, jet skiing.

The other main centre for water sports lies between Iráklion and Knossós Beach. Water-skiing is very popular here.

As for windsurfing, equipment is available for hire at various resorts, notably Ágios Nikólaos and Sitía.

Sporting possibilities are endless: skimming over the sea or, for landlubbers, marvellous hikes.

Skin-Diving

Snorkelling has a bigger following on Crete than scuba diving. The mask, fins and so on can be purchased almost anywhere, and the rocky areas to explore lie just below the surface. Even near the larger towns the water is crystal clear, the sea life amazingly varied.

You need a permit from the local police to fish with a spear gun. Most people just look at the abundant flora and fauna here. The submerged ruins around Oloús at Eloúnda and the island of Móchlos, both on the Bay of Mirabéllo, provide a field day for underwater explorers—but underwater photography is not allowed here. Though there's little chance of making any discoveries, remember that removing antiquities is strictly forbidden in Greece.

Fishing

Amateur anglers are allowed to drop their lines all along the shores and harbours. No licence is required. Deep-sea forays for the big fish are now almost non-existent.

If you're lucky enough to make a good catch, you might be able to talk a seaside *tavérna* into cooking it for your lunch.

Swimming

Everyone goes to the beach on Crete. Fortunately there's no shortage of sand here, and you can pick the spot which suits you best. Or, you can spend your sunning and swimming time at a hotel or public pool next to the sea. Along the south coast you can hire a caïque and find your own beautiful, deserted cove.

Any beach on Crete is a good beach and most are sandy. If there are dangerous currents, this is usually marked by a sign. But don't expect to find a life-guard (except at hotel beaches). Even with the facilities offered by the EOT (National Tourist Organization of Greece)—showers, changing rooms and such—you're mainly left on your own.

Going a little way to either the east or west of Iráklion, you'll find miles of beautiful, open beach. Other outstanding swimming places include the beaches at Mália, Réthymnon, Chaniá, Váï (lined with date-palms) and Falásarna on the western tip of the island.

All of Crete's beaches are public—even when they seem to belong to a hotel. Unfortunately, despite government efforts, the island's marvellous coastline is often spoiled by black tar.

NB: Sunbathing and swimming in the nude are considered punishable offences, but toplessness is very common now, except on beaches near small villages where local people object.

With luck, fresh fish for lunch; deserted beaches can still be found.

Tennis

You can hire a tennis court in Iráklion or Chaniá at a moderate rate. The Iráklion courts, located behind the Archaeological Museum, are well maintained. In both places, you can arrange to take lessons. Inquire at the tourist office or the tennis club.

Hiking and Climbing

Iráklion, Réthimnon and Chaniá have clubs which organize frequent hiking or mountain-climbing excursions (see p. 67). Foreigners are welcome to join, and the local tourist office will have the details.

If you just want to go for a walk in the country, take a bus to a place that interests you, explore the area at your leisure, then return to your starting point by bus when you're tired.

Flora...

Crete is a 12-month showcase. Spring if the ideal time, of course, but there's also a "second spring" after the start of the autumn rains. Even during the long, dry summer and in the middle of winter, Crete has an amazing array of plants and trees—more than 1,500 species, of which 182 are found only on the island.

In winter, white sprays of almond blossoms take the place of snow. Travel into the countryside to see them in late January and February. The ground below is carpeted with white narcissus, pink and lavender anemones and wild orchids of every variety.

The winter flowers continue into spring, joined by the waxy-yellow prickly pear flowers, asphodel and iris. One variety of iris with an orange stripe against a blue background is *Iris Cretensis* after the island. When orchards of orange and lemon trees blossom, the scent is overpowering, especially in the evening. The hills take on a different look, covered with bright yellow gorse and broom, and Cretan fields turn into blankets of daisies, dotted with scarlet poppies.

During summer, bougainvillea drapes over ruins and garden walls, along with the sweet-smelling jasmine and honeysuckle. White and pink oleander proliferate. On the beaches you're likely to see the tenacious sand daffodil. The gigantic candelabra of *Agave americana*, found along the roads, has a curious idiosyncrasy: it blooms once, after 10 to 15 years, and then dies. And the countryside is redolent with the flowering thyme that gives Cretan honey its distinctive flavour. Thyme and bees are inseparable here.

Heather turns the hills lavender in autumn. Cultivated gardens form a patchwork of zinnias, geraniums and chrysanthemums. With the winter rains, purple and saffron crocuses and flashy

Even in winter, you'll find the countryside alive with flowers.

Crete is a birdwatcher's paradise.

cyclamen appear. And even the oranges and lemons, which ripen in the winter, brighten the landscape.

A profusion of herbs grow on Crete. The one that has been associated with the island since antiquity is dittany, *Origanum dictamnus,* or *díktamo,* as the Cretans call it. Named after Mount Díkti, it's usually served as a herb-tea to soothe a vast number of ills.

In Minoan times, cypress trees covered the island. Since then, continual deforestation and neglect have greatly reduced the wooded area, but some cypresses remain on the western end. In some parts you'll see ilex trees and, next to every countryside *kafenío,* chestnut or plane trees for shade.

The one tree that grows everywhere is the olive. Its gnarled trunk, silvery green leaves and ripening fruit are as much a part of Crete as the Cretan himself. The olive oil from the island is justifiably famous and a major export industry. Another important tree is the carob, especially dense on the eastern part of Crete. Known also as St. John's bread because John the Baptist was supposed to have eaten it while wandering in the wilderness, its history goes back to ancient times. The bean is eaten by both humans and animals, and the gum has a wide variety of uses. Crete is the world's major exporter. The word *carat* derives from the Greek *keration* meaning "little horn"—the tough (horny) little carob bean was originally used as the standard of measure.

...and Fauna

Besides the ever-present and practical donkey, the most important animal on Crete is the wild ibex or *agrími,* also called the *kri-kri*. A large but nimble goat with sweeping horns, the *agrími* is seen only on Crete. They show up frequently in Minoan art. Until recently the *agrími* roamed the island freely. Now, to preserve them from extinction, the Gorge of Samariá and certain other areas have been designated as reserves.

The most ordinary birds—goldfinches, larks and warblers—seem exotic when seen among the Minoan ruins. In the mountains, you may catch sight of griffon vultures, falcons and eagles. The island is on the route of many migrating birds and receives annual visits from noisy flocks of swallows. You will also see lesser-known birds like the hoopoe and the bee-eater. The familiar butterfly flourishes on Crete: groups of them add a ravishing touch to the landscape.

Cypress trees once covered the island but few wooded areas remain.

Wining and Dining

Though basically Greek, the food on Crete has its own special touch. The accent is on natural, fresh flavour; the helpings are hearty. The ingredients—fruit, vegetables and meat—don't have to travel very far to your table. A morning stroll through the market-place will tell you what you're likely to find simmering in the kitchen later in the day.*

---

* The Berlitz EUROPEAN MENU READER has a comprehensive glossary of Greek wining and dining.

What many tourists remember most about Cretan cooking is the typical salad topped with black olives and *féta* cheese, next to a plate of sizzling, skewered meat kebabs *(souvlákia)*. You'll find such fare everywhere—in de luxe restaurants and in village *tavérnes*.

Very likely you'll dine outdoors under an awning, perhaps facing the sea. Unfortunately, most of the fish served probably did not come from that sea—unless the day's

Open the pots and choose your meal straight off the stove.

catch was very good. Whether from near or far, much of the seafood has become extremely expensive on Crete. If you're willing to splash out, try the *barboúnia*, red mullet that's grilled and served head and all with a wedge of lemon. Or sample the squid *(kalamarákia)* deep-fried in batter—or a heaped plate of crisp whitebait *(marídes)*. A swordfish *(xifías)* steak or kebab is a reasonably priced alternative.

Every country has its own characteristic casserole. In Greece, it's the delicious *moussaká*, layers of aubergine (eggplant), minced meat and tomato topped with white sauce. If you've selected your meal in the restaurant's kitchen—which you should—*moussaká* could well be your choice. And you'll always find chicken *(kotópoulo)*, either grilled or roasted.

Two other meat dishes frequently featured are grilled lamb chops *(païdákia)* and roast beef *(moschári psitó)*, usually served with potatoes and vegetables that have been cooked with the meat.

The fresh-baked bread on the table comes from one of those white-washed, beehive-shaped structures seen all over Crete. If you're putting together a picnic, every town market-place has its bread stand offering several shapes and sizes. Those dark rusks (zwieback) you see everywhere, called *paximádia*, look like large, flat stones. Bite into them and they're likely to feel hard as rock until you soak them a moment in water or milk. Then they become delicious. Some people like to break the rusks into bits and put them in the salad dressing.

Cretan Specialities

Each of the three sections of the island has its own culinary specialities. In central Crete, you're likely to be served an appetite-filling *stiffádo*, beef braised with onions and spices, and the classic grape leaves stuffed with rice and chopped meat, called *dolmádes*. The plump, juicy grapes from the region—if you can manage a portion—will make a refreshing finish to dinner. Iráklion is known for its *bougátsa*, a custard-filled pastry, which you'll see Cretans eating with their mid-morning coffee. If you pick up the habit too, *bougátsa* may become another one of those things you'll miss most about Crete.

Eastern Crete is best known for its fish, almost always served grilled. The Greeks pay a lot of attention to their seafood. A platter is often brought to the table from which you can select your own fish. Better still, go into the kitchen where it's kept on ice and, like a Cretan, choose the best. The fish's eyes should be bright and full, its gills red, its flesh firm and its skin glittering. Your dinner will then be put on the scale: you pay by the weight. Another speciality of eastern Crete, particularly of the town of Neápolis, is *soumáda,* a rich drink made from pressed almonds.

In the Réthimnon area of western Crete, the making of cheese is still a home industry. The cheese ranges from the soft and slightly bland *anthótyro* and *manoúri* to the harder, Gruyère-type *graviéra* —very good with grapes or on its own with drinks. *Mizíthra,* a soft, fresh cheese, is available only in winter. *Féta,* a goat-milk cheese, has become synonymous with Greek cuisine. Why not try it Cretan style, sprinkled with a little olive oil, black pepper and oregano?

From the Sfakiá mountains comes a fine dark honey, often served on yoghurt. If you're tired of the usual pastry breakfast, yoghurt with honey goes very well with your first coffee.

The Chaniá region also produces succulent oranges and tangerines. In the spring, you can find a cream cheese and mint pastry called *kaltsoúnia,* traditional Easter fare.

Snacks

Finding a quick snack any time of day is no problem at all on Crete. Almost every street has its stand and its speciality. Some sell miniature *souvlákia* on small, wooden skewers served on a slice of bread. Others have hot, flaky-crusted cheese pasties. Stands serving *gýros*—meats packed onto a vertical spit, grilled, then thinly sliced—are always popular. *Gýros* comes plain in a bread roll or Cretan-style with tomato, cucumber, onion, yoghurt and whatever else strikes the cook's fancy.

Fruit is always a good snack. In Crete, you can find an abundant selection all year round. Try some of the more unusual varieties like fresh figs, mulberries or that Cretan symbol of good luck and fertility, the pomegranate.

Restaurants

Like all Greeks, the Cretans take their dining seriously. You won't lack for restaurants on the island—the problem is choosing one. In the cities and towns, the government grades the restaurants (A, B, C and so on) depending both on facilities offered and the quality of the food. But the best indication is the other diners. If they're tourists, too, the food will probably be bland, similar to that in a hotel dining room. If the customers are mainly Cretans and foreign residents (their tans are darker than the tourists' and they speak Greek to the waiter), then the food is

A Greek salad coming right up.

more likely to be authentic and more interesting.

Even if the restaurant has a menu in a language you understand, it's a good idea to look into the kitchen and choose your meal right off the stove. The variety of Greek food is evident in the kitchens, where diners are quite welcome. It's also the place where you may learn your first Greek words. If you can't manage all that olive oil, master the phrase *chorís ládi,* meaning without oil.

Try a homemade soup to start off with. Even the most humble *tavérna* will have a pot of it simmering away on the stove. One of the best is *soúpa avgolémono,* made out of chicken stock, eggs, lemon and rice.

Never expect a quick lunch or dinner. There's no such thing on Crete. Meals are always long, pleasant affairs. Besides, with all that sunshine, the rhythm of lapping waves and the potent Cretan wine, who would want to rush? Restaurants serve lunch from about 1 until 3 p.m. and dinner from 8.30 p.m. to midnight, even later in summer. If it seems too long until the evening meal, remember that an *oúzo* and some *mezédes* can help bridge the hunger gap.

Service is always included in your bill, but most people leave a small tip in addition (from 5 to 10 per cent), if satisfied with the service.

> **The Vólta**
>
> One of the many everyday pleasures on Crete is the evening *vólta,* a more or less Mediterranean institution consisting of a promenade around the harbour or in the main square of town (in Iráklion, on Platía Eleftherías). A great social occasion, it continues until 8.30 or 9 o'clock, at which time everyone finds his favourite outdoor restaurant.
>
> The Cretans turn out for the *vólta* wearing their best. It's very important who's wearing what, who is with whom or not with whom. For some, it takes the place of a gossip column in the local paper. Others get together to discuss sport and politics. The *vólta* is also a good opportunity for the young men and women—and participating tourists—to look one another over and make some new friends.

Tavérnes

The distinction between a *tavérna* and a restaurant is no longer very clear. *Tavérnes* tend to be cheaper and have a more limited choice of food than restaurants. You'll find the relaxed atmosphere very much in keeping with seaside life. The awning is often a grape arbour or bamboo roof that lets the sunlight filter through. Most *tavérnes* have menus, with two columns: on the left, the basic price, on the right, what you pay with service and tax. If you taste the wine from the barrel, you may be pleasantly surprised by the quality of a local vintage.

In a small village, the *tavérna* will probably be the only place to eat. It's also the spot to see Cretan dancing (see p. 72).

Kafenío(n)

Definitely a male domain, the traditional *kafenío* is an extension of the Cretan's living room and office. Though no tourist would ever be turned away, he would probably be seated outdoors. Inside, the smoky room reverberates with *kombolóïa* (worry beads), the clacking of *távli* (backgammon) and everyone speaking enthusiastically at the same time.

The *kafenío* is worth visiting for the experience of drinking a cup of coffee in a uniquely Cretan setting. In larger cities, particularly on a street with heavy tourist traffic, the *kafenío* may have become just another café. If it's a *kafeníobar*, you should have a wider choice of alcoholic beverages.

Mezé

Once or twice in the course of your evening *vólta,* you'll want to sit down to rest your feet and have an *oúzo*. From a ringside seat at an outdoor café, you can continue to enjoy the *vólta*.

Greeks wisely never drink without having something to eat. You'll always receive a saucer containing a *mezé* (appetizer) with your *oúzo*. It may be only salted nuts, olives or cheese. But, if you're lucky and the establishment prides itself on its *mezé,* you might receive fried squid, cheese or spinach pasties, or stuffed grape leaves *(dolmadákia),* a small version of *dolmádes*.

Your *mezé* can easily be expanded into a full meal. But beware: the bill may add up to more than a regular dinner in a restaurant. Nonetheless, you'll have an opportunity to taste some things not generally available in restaurants. Two delicious dips often served for *mezé* are *melidzanosaláta,* a baked aubergine purée flavoured with garlic, onions and herbs, and pink *taramosaláta,* made of mullet roe and oil. Both are enhanced by squeezing lemon juice over them. In addition, you might be offered seafood like octopus, squid, prawns and iodine-flavoured, raw sea urchins. Other *mezédes* include miniature meatballs *(keftédes),* raw artichokes and many salad ingredients, to be eaten separately or mixed together.

Coffee and Desserts

After your meal—or at any time of day when you feel like having something sweet—head for the local *zacharoplastío* (pastry shop). It usually carries a selection of imitation European confections (point to your choice) and the famous Greek pastries, known as *glyká*. The most familiar is *baklavá,* thin pastry layers and chopped nuts steeped in honey. But don't leave without trying *kataífi,* a shredded-wheat and honey concoction filled with chopped nuts, or *galaktoboúreko,* a rich pastry filled with custard.

A Cretan speciality is *loukoumádes,* deep-fried batter balls doused in honey. Certain

Anise-flavoured oúzo, the national aperitif, is delightfully different.

sweet shops stack golden mounds of these Middle Eastern delights in their windows.

Cretan water is always safe to drink, if not particularly pleasant. The waiter will give you a glass with your dessert and coffee that should neutralize the sweet after-taste.

Coffee is always served Turkish style in tiny cups, already sweetened. The art of lingering long over a single cup of coffee is well developed on Crete. Once you become accustomed to the pace, you'll find yourself sitting and sipping and watching the passing scene. The coffee grounds sink to the bottom of the cup, so make sure to stop sipping in time.

Since the coffee and sugar are prepared together, you should specify how you like it. *Métrios* is for medium sweet, *varýs glykós* for very sweet. *Me olígi* means very little sugar and *skétos,* no sugar at all. If you just say coffee *(kafé),* it will arrive quite sweet.

Most cafés also serve instant coffee, called either "American" or "Nes". Espresso machines are common in tourist areas.

Wines and Spirits

Though Crete has some very pleasant wines, it's not the place for a wine connoisseur. In former times, however, this was not the case—the island was noted for its wine. Madeira even imported vine cuttings. In the 16th century, the English were singing the praises of Cretan malmsey, a sweet white wine, and drinking it widely.

Those who don't care for the taste of *retsína* (resinated wine) will be reassured to know that it's as avoidable on Crete as on the mainland. When you want unresinated wine, specify *aretsínoto*. On the other hand, you may be surprised at how well that turpentine taste goes with rich Greek food. White wine is *áspro,* red *mávro* (meaning dark) and rosé *kókkino* (literally "red", but in this case rosé).

You might like to ask for a wine from the co-operative of the Pezá region. Minos produces the best rosé on the island, and their red and white are also quite drinkable. Local wine, drier and heavier than other European varieties, may please your palate as well as your purse. The new wine tends to be rather light and mild, but by the end of the season it sometimes resembles sherry. Of course, you'll also find other—non-local—Greek wines almost everywhere you go.

As for the beer *(býra)* on sale in Greece, it has German origins and is very good indeed. Many well-known European breweries bottle beer in Greece.

Anise-flavoured *oúzo* is a powerful aperitif and a good complement to evening *mezé*. Greeks drink it straight or, on a very hot day, with an ice cube. It's also customary to add water, which turns it a milky colour.

Crete, a tangerine-growing country, also produces a delicious liqueur called *mandaríni*. For the brave, there's *rakí,* or *tsikoudiá* (the name of the Turkish equivalent of ouzo), said to be one way of telling the men from the boys. Réthimnon has an even stronger spirit, *mournorakí,* made from mulberries. Both of these are served in very small glasses, so you can proceed at your own pace.

To Help You Order

Could we have a table? **Tha boroúsame na échoume éna trapézi?**

I'd like a/an/some... **Tha íthela...**

beer	**mía býra**	mineral water	**metallikó neró**
bread	**psomí**		
coffee	**éna kafé**	potatoes	**patátes**
cutlery	**machero-pírouna**	rice	**rýzi**
		salad	**mía saláta**
dessert	**éna glykó**	serviette	**mía chartopetséta**
fish	**psári**	soup	**mía soúpa**
fruit	**froúta**	sugar	**záchari**
glass	**éna potíri**	tea	**éna tsäi**
ice-cream	**éna pagotó**	(iced) water	**(pagoméno) neró**
meat	**kréas**		
milk	**gála**	wine	**krasí**

BLUEPRINT for a Perfect Trip

How to Get There

Crete is accessible by road, rail, sea and air. Your travel agent can help you find the right combination and give you the latest information on rates and regulations. The Greek National Tourist Organization can also provide up-to-date maps and schedules to help you plan.

BY AIR

Scheduled flights

Most regularly scheduled flights change in Athens for Crete. Olympic Airways operates frequently each day to both Chaniá and Iráklion airports, each about a 45-minute trip from the Greek capital.

Charter flights and package tours

From the U.K. and Ireland: Several large companies offer tours through travel agents. Prices vary enormously depending on accommodation and extras. You might consider a "theme" holiday, such as a botanical or archaeological tour, or a "keep fit" sports package. A tour operator can also give details on "Wanderer" holidays for travellers planning a walking tour, using vouchers for accommodation in inexpensive youth hostels and boarding houses.

From North America: Charter flights and package tours which include Crete in their programmes are widely available. There are straightforward flight/hotel arrangements, and packages featuring Crete as part of "Classical Greece" tours, often with cruise add-on.

BY ROAD

For motorists, the preferred itinerary from northern Europe is via Munich, Belgrade and Niš to Salonica in northern Greece. You can reduce time by loading yourself and your car on an auto-train for part of the journey (expensive) or by driving through France and Italy and taking one of the Italy–Greece ferries for the final stage of the trip: car ferries operate between Ancona and Iráklion on Crete and more frequently between certain other Italian ports and mainland Greece.

BY RAIL

From Paris, there are two main routes (although a number of variations are possible): the cheaper route is via Simplon, Venice, Ljubljana,

Belgrade and Salonica. The other, more expensive, route goes via Bologna, Brindisi and Patras (the fare includes ferry crossing Brindisi–Patras). The latter route is by far the most popular.

Anyone under 26 can purchase an *Inter-Rail Card* which allows one month of unlimited 2nd-class rail travel on all participating European railways. The *Rail Europ S Card,* obtainable before departure only, entitles senior citizens to purchase train tickets for European destinations at reduced prices. Anyone living outside Europe and North Africa can purchase a *Eurailpass* before leaving home. People intending to undertake a lot of rail travel once in Greece may like to buy a *Greek Tourist Card* which is available for unlimited 2nd-class travel over the lines of the Greek Railways.

BY SEA

Cargo/passenger services are available from the U.S. to Piraeus in Greece. Departures are approximately three to four times per month with dates and ports of call subject to cargo requirements.

There are also cargo/passenger services from Southampton to Piraeus. The duration of the voyage is approximately 10 days.

During peak season, there are many sailings each week from Piraeus to Iráklion (a 12-hour voyage) and Chaniá (11 hours). A daily car-ferry service operates between Iráklion and Piraeus and between Chaniá and Piraeus.

When to Go

Crete enjoys a good climate throughout the year and is becoming increasingly popular as a winter destination for tourists fleeing the cold. Even in January and February, the coolest months, the temperature seldom drops below 46° Fahrenheit.

		J	F	M	A	M	J	J	A	S	O	N	D
Iráklion air temperatures*	Max. °F	60	60	64	70	76	82	86	86	82	78	70	66
	°C	16	16	18	21	24	28	30	30	28	26	21	19
	Min. °F	48	48	50	54	60	64	68	72	68	62	68	52
	°C	9	9	10	12	16	18	20	22	20	17	14	11
Sea temperatures*	°F	61	61	63	64	68	73	75	77	75	73	66	63
	°C	16	16	17	18	20	23	24	25	24	23	19	17

*Approximate monthly averages

Facts and Figures

Although much of the information given below can be found in various sections of our guide, key facts are grouped here for a quick briefing.

Geography: Crete *(Kríti)* is Greece's southernmost and largest island with an area of about 8,300 square kilometres (3,200 square miles), and the fifth largest island in the Mediterranean after Sicily, Sardinia, Cyprus and Corsica. It lies some 260 km. (160 miles) south of Athens and 320 km. (200 miles) north of Libya. The highest point is Mount Ídi (or Psilorítis) at 2,456 metres (8,058 feet).

Population: ca. 500,000.

Major towns: Iráklion (110,000), Chaniá (50,000), Réthimnon (20,000), Ágios Nikólaos (6,000).

Government: Greece is a presidential parliamentary republic. The country is divided into 10 regions, which are subdivided into more than 50 administrative districts or prefectures *(nomí)*, of which Crete comprises four: Iráklion, Chaniá, Réthimnon and Lasíthi. Each *nomós* is administered by a local governor or nomarch who is appointed by the central government in Athens, and each *nomós* is represented in Parliament by deputies, the number depending on the population of each individual district.

Economy: Crete's main sources of income are tourism and agricultural products (olives, grapes, vegetables). Main exports: olives and olive oil, grapes, raisins, wine, citrus fruits.

Religion: More than 95% of Greeks belong to the Orthodox Church, under the Patriarch of Constantinople and Archbishop of Athens. The Cretan Church is administratively autonomous and headed by the Archbishop of Crete.

Planning Your Budget

To give you an idea of what to expect, here are some average prices in Greek drachmas. However, due to inflation all prices must be regarded as *approximate*.

Babysitters. 1,000–1,500 drs. per hour.

Bicycle rental. 400–550 drs. per day, 2,750–3,850 drs. per week.

Camping. Average prices per day: adults 250–750 drs., children (up to 10) up to 300 drs., tents 125–600 drs., cars 65–320 drs., caravans (trailers) 125–750 drs.

Car rental (international company, high season July–Oct.). *Subaru 600* 3,025 drs. per day, 44 drs. per km., 57,860 drs. per week with unlimited mileage. *Opel Kadett 1.2* 3,475 drs. per day, 47 drs. per km., 63,820 drs. per week with unlimited mileage. Add 16% tax.

Cigarettes. Local brands 135–240 drs. per packet of 20, foreign brands 200–600 drs.

Entertainment. *Bouzoúki* evening, including food 3,500 drs. and up, discotheque usually free entrance with high drink charges, cinema 250–400 drs.

Hairdressers. *Man's* haircut 1,500 drs., shave 200–350 drs. *Woman's* haircut 700–1,500, shampoo and set or blow-dry 800–3,000 drs., permanent wave 3,500–6,000 drs.

Hotels (double room with bath, summer season). De luxe 18,000–33,000 drs., class A 10,000–19,000 drs., class B 8,000–13,000 drs., class C 4,000–7,000 drs., class D 2,000–3,000 drs.

Meals and drinks. Continental breakfast 250–500 drs., lunch or dinner in fairly good establishment 1,500–2,800 drs., coffee 120–300 drs., Greek brandy 100–350 drs., gin and tonic 350–550 drs., beer 100–200 drs., soft drink 60–250 drs.

Shopping bag. Bread (½ kg.) 65 drs., butter (250 g.) 260 drs., 6 eggs 120 drs., *féta* cheese (½ kg.) 400 drs., potatoes (1 kg.) 60 drs., minced meat (1 kg.) 1,000 drs., soft drinks (small bottle) 60 drs.

Sports. Pedalo boat 350–550 drs. per hour. Water-skiing 3,300 drs. for ten minutes. Windsurfing 800–3,500 drs. per hour.

Youth hostels. 560–1,250 drs. per night.

An A–Z Summary of Practical Information and Facts

> Listed after most main entries is an appropriate Greek translation, usually in the singular. You'll find this vocabulary useful when asking for information or assistance.
>
> A star (*) following an entry indicates that relevant prices are to be found on page 101.

A

AIRPORT *(aerodrómio)*. Crete has three airports, the major one near Iráklion (5 km. from the town) and the others near Chaniá (15 km. from the town) and Sitía. Apart from a few charters, Chaniá airport is used for domestic Greek flights only and has limited facilities, while the Sitía field accommodates small charter craft.

All international flights arrive at Iráklion airport. Here, members of charter or package-tour groups will be shepherded through customs with a minimum of formalities, they, together with their luggage, being in general transferred directly from plane to waiting coach to resort hotel. Porters are available for the individual traveller.

There's a duty-free shop at Iráklion, and you'll find a restaurant, snack-bar, car-hire firms and travel-agency counters. Public and airport buses provide services to town and taxis are plentiful.

Porter!	**Achthofóre!**
Taxi!	**Taxi!**
Where's the bus for…?	**Pou íne to leoforío giá…?**

ALPHABET. See also LANGUAGE, and box on page 24. The exotic letters of the Greek alphabet needn't be a mystery to you. The table below lists the Greek letters in their capital and small forms, followed by the letters they correspond to in English.

Stress, a very important feature of the Greek language, is indicated in our transcription by an accent mark (´) above the vowel of the syllable to be emphasized. Accentuate the wrong syllable and you may evoke puzzlement or total misunderstanding in your listener.

A	α	a	as in b**a**r		Ξ	ξ	x	like **ks** in than**ks**
B	β	v			O	o	o	as in b**o**ne
Γ	γ	g	as in **g**o*		Π	π	p	
Δ	δ	d	like **th** in **th**is		P	ρ	r	
E	ε	e	as in g**e**t		Σ	σ, ς	s	as in ki**ss**
Z	ζ	z			T	τ	t	
H	η	i	like **ee** in m**ee**t		Y	υ	i	like **ee** in m**ee**t
Θ	θ	th	as in **th**in		Φ	φ	f	
I	ι	i	like **ee** in m**ee**t		X	χ	ch	as in Scottish lo**ch**
K	κ	k			Ψ	ψ	ps	as in ti**ps**y
Λ	λ	l			O/Ω	ω	o	as in b**o**ne
M	μ	m						
N	ν	n			OY	ου	ou	as in s**ou**p

* except before **i**- and **e**-sounds, when it's pronounced like **y** in **y**es

ANTIQUITIES *(archéa)*. Antiquities may be exported only with the approval of the Archaeological Council and the Greek Ministry of Culture and Science. Lawbreakers face a stiff fine and a prison sentence of up to five years. So if you stumble upon an ancient amphora or buy a "genuine Byzantine icon", you should contact the head of the local museum, who will tell you if you may take it home and the correct procedure to follow.

BABYSITTERS* *("baby-sitter")*. We suggest you check with your hotel receptionist or your travel-agency representative. Note that children are accepted anywhere at any time on Crete; most Cretans take their children with them whenever they go out, even to late-night restaurants.

Can you get us a babysitter for tonight?	**Boríte na mas vríte mía "baby-sitter" gi'apópse?**

BICYCLE and MOTORSCOOTER RENTAL* *(enikiásis podiláton/ motopodiláton)*. In all the tourist centres there are firms that hire out bicycles, motorscooters and mopeds (motorbikes) (though you may have to queue up for a bicycle on Sundays and public holidays). Moped rental charges are about two-thirds those of motorscooters.

B **BUSES** *(leoforío)*. In general, buses are dependable and punctual. Besides the frequent services connecting Iráklion, Ágios Nikólaos, Réthimnon and Chaniá, buses also serve practically every village and archaeological site on the island. The vehicles—much more robust than they may appear at first sight—manage to get you to some very out-of-the-way places. The sign for a bus-stop is ΣΤΑΣΙΣ *(stásis)*. Though passengers are supposed to purchase their tickets in advance, last-minute sprinters will be able to pay the driver. Hold on to your ticket, as inspectors occasionally board buses to check the paperwork.

When's the next bus to…?	**Póte févgi to epómeno leoforío giá…?**
single (one-way)	**apló**
return (round-trip)	**me epistrofí**

C **CAMPING*** (ΚΑΜΠΙΝΓΚ—*"camping"*). There are about a dozen official campsites on the island, open May to September. The tourist office will provide you with all the particulars.

May we camp here?	**Boroúme na kataskinósoume edó?**
We've a tent.	**Échoume mía skiní.**
Can I hire/buy a sleeping bag?	**Boró na nikiáso/agoráso éna "sleeping-bag"?**

CAR RENTAL* (ΕΝΟΙΚΙΑΣΕΙΣ ΑΥΤΟΚΙΝΗΤΩΝ—*enikiásis aftokiníton*). Local companies, with limited vehicle parks but negotiable rates, vie with the internationally known car-hire companies for your trade. During the high season, it's wise to reserve at least a day in advance.

Many agencies demand a deposit equivalent to the estimated total cost of your rental, though this requirement is waived in the case of major credit-card holders. Third-party liability insurance is often included in the rate, and complete coverage is available for a modest extra charge. All rates are subject to stamp duty and local taxes. Off season, you may expect a reduction.

The law requires an International Driving Permit for all foreigners *hiring* a car in Greece, though in practice the car-rental agencies accept any valid national licence that has been held for at least one year. Minimum age for renting a car is 23.

I'd like to rent a car tomorrow.	**Tha íthela na nikiáso éna aftokínito ávrio.**
for one day/a week	**giá mía iméra/mía evdomáda**

CHURCH SERVICES *(litourgía)*. The national religion of Greece is the Greek Orthodox faith. There are no Anglican or other Protestant services held on Crete, nor is there a Jewish congregation. Mass is said on Saturdays, Sundays and holy days at the Catholic church in Iráklion, on Patrós Antoníou, in Chaniá at the Catholic church on Chálidon, as well as in the Catholic churches of Rethimnon and Ágios Nikólaos.

What time is mass?	**Ti óra archízi i litourgía?**

CIGARETTES, CIGARS, TOBACCO* *(tsigára; poúra; kapnós)*. The sign to look for is ΚΑΠΝΟΠΩΛΕΙΟ—*kapnopolío* (tobacconist's). Greek tobacco, most of it coming from Macedonia, is world-famous, and provided you stick to local products you'll find that smoking is a bargain in Greece. Local cigarettes range from very strong, unfiltered varieties to quite mild, filtered brands. *Astor* and *Old Navy* are popular, as is the menthol-flavoured *Mistral*. Most leading foreign cigarettes are available, but at two to three times the price of local brands. Dutch and American small cigars can also be purchased.

A packet of cigarettes/matches.	**Éna pakéto tsigára/spírta.**
filter-tipped/without filter	**me/chorís fíltro**
light/dark tobacco	**xanthós/mávros kapnós**

CLOTHING *(rouchismós)*. Crete is both informal and—especially in summer—warm, so the average visitor won't need an extensive wardrobe. But do bring a light sweater along for the evening. (If you're travelling by boat, particularly in winter, a warm anorak or coat is a necessity.) For more formal evening wear, you may want to pack a long dress or light sports coat.

On the beach, toplessness is acceptable almost everywhere, except near small villages where local people object. However, when you're walking to and from bathing areas, slip on a shirt or cover-up.

When visiting churches, be sure to dress respectfully.

Cotton is preferable to synthetic materials in the hot weather. A wide-brimmed hat is also recommendable. To protect your feet against the burning sands or pebble beaches, a pair of sandals is a good investment. Those produced on the island are well made and cheap. A comfortable pair of sturdy shoes is sensible when clambering around historical sites or hiking and essential if you intend to explore the Samariá Gorge.

The following chart gives clothing sizes in case you're shopping:

Women								
Clothing			Shirts	Pullovers		Shoes		
GB	USA	Greece	GB	USA	Greece	GB	USA	Greece
10	8	40	32	10	42	3	4½	35
12	10	42	34	12	44	4	5½	36
14	12	44	36	14	46	5	6½	37
16	14	46	38	16	48	6	7½	38
18	16	48	40	18	50	7	8½	39

Men						
Clothing		Shirts		Shoes		
GB / USA	Greece	GB / USA	Greece	GB	USA	Greece
36	46	14	36	6	6½	39
38	48	14½	37	7	7½	40
40	50	15	38	8	8½	41
42	52	15½	39	9	9½	42
44	54	16	40	10	10½	43

Will I need a jacket and tie?	**Tha chriastó sakáki ke graváta?**
Is it all right if I wear this?	**Tha íme endáxi an foréso aftó?**

COMPLAINTS *(parápona)*. Although consumer protection is in its infancy in this country, Greeks are firm believers in fair play in commercial affairs. If you really feel you've been cheated or misled, raise the matter with the manager or proprietor of the establishment in question first.

If you still feel you have not been honestly dealt with, then take the problem to the tourist police (see POLICE).

CONSULATES and EMBASSIES *(proxenío; presvía)*. Several countries have consulates in Iráklion. All embassies are in Athens. Hours vary so it's best to call first.

British consulate:* Papalexándrou 16, Iráklion; tel.: 22 40 12 and 23 41 27.

Canadian embassy: Gennadíou 4, Ypsilántou, 115-21 Athens; tel.: 723 95 11.

U.S. embassy: Leofóros Vas. Sofías 91, 101-60 Athens; tel.: 721 29 51.

If you run into any difficulties with the authorities or the police, get in touch with your consulate for advice.

Where's the British/American/ Canadian consulate?	Pou íne to anglikó/amerikanikó/ kanadikó proxenío?

CONVERSION TABLES. For tire pressure, distance and fluid measures—see page 111. Greece uses the metric system.

Temperature

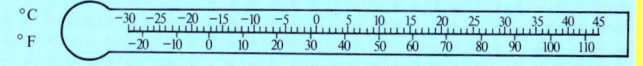

Length

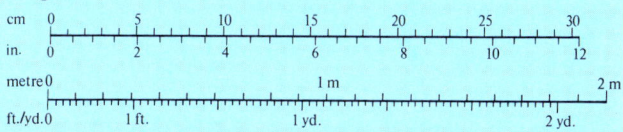

Weight

COURTESIES. Greek hospitality is sincere and generous. Especially on Crete, its lavishness can become overwhelming. Whatever you do, don't refuse it.

Don't turn down an offer of coffee and the inevitable glass of water unless it's obvious somebody is trying hard to sell you something. Should you find yourself in a Greek home, particularly in a village,

---

* Also for citizens of Eire and Commonwealth countries not separately represented.

C expect to be lavishly plied with both food and drink—and don't feel ill at ease if only you are served while your hostess looks on; it's a traditional expression of hospitality.

Greeks, in common with most continental Europeans, wish each other "bon appetit" before starting a meal. In Greek, the expression is *kalí órexi!* A common toast when drinking is *stin ygiá sas!* meaning "Cheers!". A reply to any toast, *epísis!* means "the same to you".

Staring isn't considered rude in Greece. On the contrary, it's a way of passing a compliment or satisfying curiosity (a common Greek trait), and it means no harm at all. Don't be surprised if you're asked personal questions about the size of your family or how much you earn—it's the Greeks' genuine curiosity and interest at work.

Photography can be a joy on Crete, and, though most Cretans love having their picture taken, don't fail to ask their permission first.

A major "don't": avoid waving your hand with the palm facing outwards. Greeks call this gesture *moúntsa*, and it is considered offensive. So be very careful not to spoil a pleasant encounter by waving good-bye the wrong way. Furthermore, when you use your fingers for counting, be sure to present the *back* of your hand—never the palm—to the other person; even an innocent slip could horrify a Greek, particularly in the villages.

Like the Spanish *mañana*, the Greek *ávrio* does not necessarily mean tomorrow but, rather, soon. Learn to take your time and smile. If you try to rush a Greek, it may worsen the delay.

The simple courtesies mean a lot on Crete and not only win friends but smooth your own way. It's a good idea and a simple matter to learn a few basic expressions, such as good morning *(kaliméra)*, please *(parakaló)*, thank you *(efcharistó)* and you're welcome *(típota)*. See also LANGUAGE.

CRIME and THEFT *(églima; klopí)*. You'll be glad to know that crime is practically non-existent on Crete. If you've left something valuable in a shop or restaurant, the proprietor is sure to be searching just as hard for you as you are for the article. Honesty is a matter of pride among the Greeks. Yet it's only common sense to lock up your valuables and watch your handbag in crowds—not because of the Greeks, but perhaps because of your fellow-tourists...

I want to report a theft. **Thélo na katangílo mía klopí.**

CUSTOMS CONTROLS and ENTRY FORMALITIES. Visitors from EEC (Common Market) countries only need an identity card to enter Greece. Citizens of most other countries must be in possession of a valid passport. Though European and North American residents are not subject to any health requirements, visitors from further afield may require a smallpox vaccination. Check with your travel agent before departure.

The following chart shows the quantities of certain major items you may take into Greece and, upon your return home, into your own country:

Into:	Cigarettes		Cigars		Tobacco	Spirits		Wine
Greece 1)	300	or	75	or	400 g.	1½ l.	and	5 l.
2)	200	or	50	or	250 g.	1 l.	or	2 l.
3)	400	or	100	or	500 g.	see 1)	and	2)
Canada	200	and	50	and	900 g.	1.1 l.	or	1.1 l.
Eire	200	or	50	or	250 g.	1 l.	and	2 l.
U.K.	200	or	50	or	250 g.	1 l.	and	2 l.
U.S.A.	200	and	100	or	4)	1 l.	or	1 l.

1) Residents of Europe, non-duty-free items purchased in EEC countries (alcoholic beverage allowances—also for non-European residents)
2) Residents of Europe, items purchased outside EEC countries or in EEC countries duty-free (alcoholic beverage allowances—also for non-European residents)
3) Residents outside Europe
4) A reasonable quantity

Certain prescription drugs, including tranquillizers and headache preparations, cannot be carried into the country without a prescription or official medical document. Fines—even jail sentences—have been imposed on the unwary tourist.

Currency restrictions: Non-residents may import up to 100,000 drachmas and export up to 20,000 drachmas (in denominations no larger than 5,000 drachmas). There is no limit on the foreign currency or traveller's cheques you may import or export, though amounts in excess of $1,000 or its equivalent should be declared to the customs official upon arrival so you can take them out when you leave.

I've nothing to declare.	**Den écho na dilóso típota.**

D   DRIVING IN GREECE

Entering Greece: To bring your car into Greece you'll need:

International Driving Permit (see below)	Car registration papers	Insurance coverage (the Green Card is no longer obligatory within the EEC, but comprehensive coverage is advisable)
	nationality plate or sticker	

The International Driving Permit (not required for holders of a British licence) can be obtained through your home motoring association.

The Greek Automobile Association (ELPA) will tow your car away in the event of breakdowns or other difficulties.

The standard European red warning triangle is required in Greece for emergencies. It's obligatory to use seat belts, and fines for non-compliance are high. Motorcycle and motorscooter drivers—as well as passengers—must wear crash helmets.

Driving conditions on Crete: The main road which extends across the north coast, connecting all the major towns, is broad and well-maintained. Even during the high tourist season, traffic on it is not particularly heavy. At the eastern end, your attention may be torn between the spectacular scenery and the equally spectacular hairpin bends of the road—drivers beware!

Off the national highway, the secondary roads are usually in good driving condition, though if you're travelling to any of the more remote areas, it might be more worth your while to take a bus.

Always use your horn going around curves. Greeks blast away and will expect the same from oncoming traffic. On the country roads, and even on the national highway, keep an eye out for sheep which may be crossing in front of you or have merely strayed. When passing through villages, and even in the towns, be warned that many of the older Cretans haven't really adjusted to the new age of traffic. Right-of-way seems to be a matter of whoever gets there first with drivers, and pedestrians do *not* have priority.

Traffic police: Patrol cars are easily recognizable by the word POLICE in large letters on the doors. They are particularly severe on speeding and illegal parking and may fine you on the spot for such offenses as these.

Fuel and oil: Service stations are plentiful on the island, but it's best to check your tank before heading for the more remote areas in the south. Unleaded petrol (gas) is available in Iráklion and Chaniá.

Fluid measures

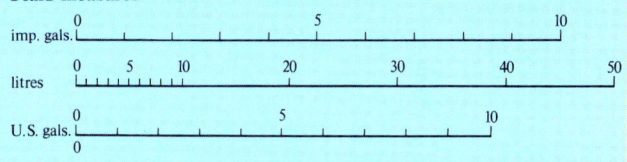

Tire pressure

lb./sq. in.	kg/cm²	lb./sq. in.	kg/cm²
10	0.7	26	1.8
12	0.8	27	1.9
15	1.1	28	2.0
18	1.3	30	2.1
20	1.4	33	2.3
21	1.5	36	2.5
23	1.6	38	2.7
24	1.7	40	2.8

Distance

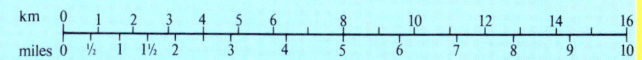

Road signs: Most road signs are the standard pictographs used throughout Europe. However, you may encounter the following written signs on Crete:

ΑΔΙΕΞΟΔΟΣ	No through road
ΑΛΤ	Stop
ΑΝΩΜΑΛΙΑ ΟΔΟΣΤΡΩΜΑΤΟΣ	Bad road surface
ΑΠΑΓΟΡΕΥΕΤΑΙ Η ΑΝΑΜΟΝΗ	No waiting
ΑΠΑΓΟΡΕΥΕΤΑΙ Η ΕΙΣΟΔΟΣ	No entry
ΑΠΑΓΟΡΕΥΕΤΑΙ Η ΣΤΑΘΜΕΥΣΙΣ	No parking
ΔΙΑΒΑΣΙΣ ΠΕΖΩΝ	Pedestrian crossing
ΕΛΑΤΤΩΣΑΤΕ ΤΑΧΥΤΗΤΑΝ	Reduce speed
ΕΠΙΚΙΝΔΥΝΟΣ ΚΑΤΩΦΕΡΕΙΑ	Dangerous incline

D

ΕΡΓΑ ΕΠΙ ΤΗΣ ΟΔΟΥ	Roadworks in progress (Men working)
ΚΙΝΔΥΝΟΣ	Caution
ΜΟΝΟΔΡΟΜΟΣ	One-way traffic
ΠΑΡΑΚΑΜΠΤΗΡΙΟΣ	Diversion (Detour)
ΠΟΔΗΛΑΤΑΙ	Cyclists
ΠΟΡΕΙΑ ΥΠΟΧΡΕΩΤΙΚΗ ΔΕΞΙΑ	Keep right
ΣΤΑΣΙΣ ΛΕΩΦΟΡΕΙΟΥ	Bus stop
(International) Driving Licence	**(diethnís) ádia odigíseos**
car registration papers	**ádia kykloforías**
Green Card	**asfália aftokinítou**
Are we on the right road for…?	**Ímaste sto sostó drómo giá…?**
Fill her up, please, top grade.	**Na to gemísete me venzíni soúper, parakaló.**
Check the oil/tires/battery.	**Na elénxete ta ládia/ta lásticha/ ti bataría.**
I've had a breakdown.	**Épatha mía vlávi.**
There's been an accident.	**Égine éna dystýchima.**

E **ELECTRIC CURRENT** *(ilektrikó révma)*. You'll find only 220-volt, 50-cycle A.C. on Crete. If you need a plug adaptor check with your hotel receptionist.

an adaptor	**énas metaschimatistís**
a battery	**mía bataría**

EMERGENCIES. Depending on the nature of the emergency, refer to the separate entries in this section such as Consulates, Health, Police, etc.

The telephone number throughout the island for any kind of emergency is 100. Though we hope you'll never need them, here are a few words you might want to learn in advance:

Careful	**Prosochí**
Fire	**Fotiá**
Help	**Voíthia**
Police	**Astynomía**
Stop	**Stamatíste**
Stop thief	**Stamatíste to kléfti**

GUIDES and INTERPRETERS *(xenagós; dierminéas)*. If you're interested in knowledgeable guidance at sites, the tourist information office can refer you to an officially recognized guide. An English-speaking guide can be hired at short notice.

We'd like an English-speaking guide.	**Tha thélame éna xenagó na milá i angliká.**
I need an English interpreter.	**Chriázome éna ánglo dierminéa.**

HAIRDRESSERS* (ΚΟΜΜΩΤΗΡΙΟ—*kommotírio*); **BARBERS** (ΚΟΥ-ΡΕΙΟ—*kourío*). On Crete you'll find hairdressers in all the popular tourist centres. You may have to book ahead of time during busy periods.

Not too much off (here).	**Óchi polý kondá (edó).**
A little more off (here).	**Lígo pió kondá (edó).**

HEALTH and MEDICAL CARE. With Crete's climate and adequate standards of hygiene, most tourists who become ill have only themselves to blame. Too much sun, food or drink—more likely a combination of all three—have ruined many a holiday. The motto is moderation.

To be completely at your ease, take out health insurance to cover the risk of illness and accident while on holiday. Your insurance representative or travel agent at home will be able to advise you. On the spot, you can turn to a Greek insurance company. Though emergency treatment is free, with insurance coverage you'll get much better medical attention if you need to be hospitalized. There's a shortage, however, of experienced medical personnel, so you may have a little difficulty getting an appointment with one of the island's doctors.

Do your eyes a favour and wear sunglasses. The famous clear light of Greece and the bright sunshine make an even more potent combination on the beaches.

Chemists' shops, or **drugstores** (ΦΑΡΜΑΚΕΙΟ—*farmakío*). You can recognize a *farmakío* by the sign hanging outside—a red or blue cross on a white background. There's always one on 24-hour duty in each main town.

Though these establishments are reasonably well stocked, you may find that your favourite brand of toothpaste or shade of nail varnish

H isn't available. For import of prescription drugs to Greece, see Customs Controls and Entry Formalities.

a doctor	énas giatrós
a dentist	énas odontogiatrós
an ambulance	éna asthenofóro
hospital	nosokomío
an upset stomach	varystomachiá
sunstroke	ilíasi
a fever	pyretós

HITCH-HIKING *(oto-stóp)*. It's legal everywhere in Greece, and you shouldn't run into too many difficulties obtaining a lift.

Can you give me a lift to...?   **Boríte na me páte méchri to...?**

HOTELS and ACCOMMODATION* (ΞΕΝΟΔΟΧΕΙΟ; ΔΩΜΑΤΙΑ— *xenodochío; domátia*). Accommodation on Crete ranges from the simplest peasant-style room in a village house to a luxury resort hotel-bungalow complex. Hotels are listed in a comprehensive index, giving prices, which can be consulted at Greek national tourist offices abroad as well as at many travel agents'.

If you're travelling individually and are unable to find a room, ask the local tourist office for help. No matter where you are or what time of the day or night it may be, room will always be found for you—it's part of Greek hospitality.

Hotels on Crete are divided into 6 categories: de luxe, A, B, C, D and E. Prices are government controlled. When air-conditioning is provided, a slight extra charge will be added to the bill. Your room rates must be displayed somewhere in your room. During the high season, the hotel management may insist on your taking at least half board. Reductions can usually be arranged for children.

Less expensive than hotels, pensions are classified as follows: A, B and C.

Private accommodation is also widely available. In every town and village you will see signs reading "rent a room" (in English). Rates are lower than at hotels. You may generally avail yourself of cooking facilities, and a bath or shower will be on the premises.

Youth Hostels (ΞΕΝΩΝ ΝΕΟΤΗΤΟΣ—*xenón neótitos*). There are youth hostels in most of the popular holiday resorts. Accommodation is simple but clean. A stay is often limited to five days. Before leaving home, apply to your national Youth Hostels Association for an international membership card. If you come undocumented, a youth hostel may let you in, but then again it may not. The Greek headquarters at Dragatsaníou 4, Athens (on Platía Klafthmónos) also issues cards.

a double/single room with/without bath	éna dipló/monó domátio me/chorís bánio
What's the rate per night?	Piá íne i timí giá mía nýkta?

HOURS. Napping, or at least reducing one's activity during the heat of the day, is a sensible old Mediterranean custom. You'll find that almost everything is closed between 1.30 and 4 or 5 p.m., and noise is very much frowned upon during those hours. Work resumes again after the siesta until around 9 p.m.

The following list gives some opening hours:

Banks: In general 8 a.m. to 2 p.m., Monday to Friday. In summer at least one bank normally remains open in larger towns between 5 and 7 p.m. and short periods on Saturdays for money changing only.

Cinemas: Two shows nightly, 8 to 10 p.m. and 10 to 12 p.m.

Museums and Sites: See pp. 75–76.

Post Offices: Main branches 7.40 a.m. to 8.30 p.m. Monday to Saturday; though hours are more irregular in villages.

Restaurants: Lunch from 1 to 3 p.m., dinner from 8.30 to midnight.

Shops: See p. 76.

LANGUAGE. See also ALPHABET. You're unlikely to have much of a language problem on Crete. Most people whose job brings them in contact with foreign tourists speak some English. Road signs are written in both Greek and Latin alphabets, and some restaurants have menus printed in several languages, including English.

The Greeks actually have two languages—the classical *katharévousa,* until recently the language of the courts and parliament and still used by a few conservative newspapers, and *dimotikí,* the spoken language and now also the official one. This is what you'll hear in

L Greece today. Though the Cretans have their own accent and a few special expressions, their language is not really very different from mainland Greek.

Good morning	**kaliméra**
Good afternoon	**kalispéra**
Good night	**kalinýkta**
Thank you	**efcharistó**
You're welcome	**típota**
Please	**parakaló**
Goodbye	**chérete**

The Berlitz phrase book GREEK FOR TRAVELLERS covers almost all situations you're likely to encounter in your travels in Greece.

LAUNDRY and DRY-CLEANING (ΠΛΥΝΤΗΡΙΟ; ΚΑΘΑΡΙΣΤΗΡΙΟ —*plyntírio; katharistírio*). In July and August, allow three or four days for a suit or dress to be dry-cleaned (at other times of the year, it will take only two days). Same-day service is available at extra cost.

The local laundry service is adequate, but delicate colours may come back faded.

When will it be ready?	**Póte tha íne étimo?**
I must have this for tomorrow morning.	**Prépi na íne étimo ávrio to proí.**

LOST and FOUND PROPERTY; LOST CHILDREN. If you've lost or mislaid something, you have a very good chance of getting it back. Check with the tourist police located in every town (see POLICE).

Children are very pampered throughout Greece and lost children are never neglected. If you really think your child has vanished, go to the tourist police. They'll probably discover the youngster at a local café being fed and interviewed by friendly Greeks.

I've lost my wallet/handbag/passport.	**Échasa to portofóli mou/ti tsánda mou/to diavatirió mou.**

M **MAIL.** If you don't know ahead of time where you'll be staying, you can have your mail addressed to poste restante, or general delivery, in whichever town is most convenient. You can pick up your mail from

7.40 a.m. until 8.30 p.m. Monday to Friday. Take your passport with you to the post office for identification. Address your mail this way:

> Mr. John Smith
> Poste Restante
> Iráklion, Crete
> Greece

Have you received any mail for...?	**Échete grámmata giá...?**

MAPS. The best and most accurate maps of Crete are produced by Mathioulákis Publications and by Christoforákis. Published in English using the Roman alphabet, these maps are available in shops on Crete and in Athens. Most car-hire companies provide you with simplified road maps, but these are inadequate for anyone wishing to explore the by-ways of Crete.

The maps in this book were prepared by Falk-Verlag, Hamburg.

a street plan of...	**éna odikó chárti tou...**
a road map of the island	**éna chárti tou nisioú**

MONEY MATTERS. The monetary unit of Greece is the drachma (*drachmí*, abbreviated Δρχ.).

Coins: 1, 2, 5, 10, 20, 50 drachmas.

Banknotes: 50, 100, 500, 1,000, 5,000 drachmas.

For currency restrictions, see CUSTOMS CONTROLS AND ENTRY FORMALITIES.

Banks and Currency-Exchange Offices (ΤΡΑΠΕΖΑ—*trápeza;* ΣΥΝΑΛ-ΛΑΓΜΑ—*sinállagma*). The major Greek banks have branch offices in Crete. You'll normally receive a better exchange rate in banks than elsewhere, especially shops or restaurants. Major brands of traveller's cheques are widely accepted, and banks or currency-exchange offices will give you a somewhat better rate than for cash. Note that the main post offices also provide currency exchange facilities. Always take your passport with you when you go to exchange money or to cash traveller's cheques. See also HOURS.

Credit Cards *(pistotikí kárta)* are honoured by major shops in large towns and by banks, car-hire firms and leading hotels displaying the card company decal.

M

Where's the nearest bank/the nearest currency-exchange office?	Pou íne i kodinóteri trápeza/to kodinótero grafío sinallágmatos?
I want to change some pounds/dollars.	Thélo na alláxo merikés líres/meriká dollária.
What's the exchange rate?	Pía íne i timí sinallágmatos?
Do you accept traveller's cheques?	Pérnete "traveller's cheques"?
Can I pay with this credit card?	Boró na pliróso me aftí ti pistotikí kárta?
Is there an admission charge?	Prépi na pliróso ísodo?
How much?	Póso káni?
Have you something cheaper?	Échete káti ftinótero?

N

NEWSPAPERS and MAGAZINES *(efimerída; periodikó)*. Most foreign dailies—including the principal British newspapers and the Paris-based *International Herald Tribune*—arrive on Crete one day late. For faster news in English, you can pick up the *Athens News*.

Have you any English-language newspapers?	Échete anglikés efimerídes?
Where can I buy English-language books?	Pou boró na agoráso angliká vivlía?

P

PETS. In view of the stringent quarantine regulations (up to 6 months) for animals now in force in Great Britain, Eire and Canada, few short-term visitors will contemplate taking a pet dog or cat along to Crete. Moreover, most hotels don't allow animals.

PHOTOGRAPHY *(fotografía)*. A photo shop is advertised by the sign ΦΩΤΟΓΡΑΦΕΙΟ *(fotografío)*. Leading brands of film are readily available, if rather expensive. Colour and black-and-white films are processed locally in from three to five days, but colour slides must be sent to the mainland.

Hand-held photo equipment may be used in all museums and on archaeological sites, but you may have to pay a fee for the camera. For tripods you have to obtain official permission since they're considered the mark of a professional, not of an amateur, photographer.

For security reasons, it's illegal to use a telephoto lens aboard an aircraft flying over Greece. But there are no restrictions on ordinary still and ciné-cameras. Photography is forbidden around Iráklion airport and in the entire Soúda Bay area.

Photo shops sell lead-coated plastic bags which protect films from x-rays at airport security checkpoints.

I'd like a film for this camera.	**Tha íthela éna film giaftí ti michaní.**
black-and-white film	**asprómavro film**
colour prints	**énchromo film**
35-mm film	**éna film triánda pénde milimétr**
colour slides	**énchromo film giá sláïds**
super-8	**soúper-októ**
How long will it take to develop (and print) this film?	**Se póses iméres boríte na emfanísete (ke na ektypósete) aftó to film?**

POLICE *(astynomía)*. There are two kinds of police on Crete. Regular policemen are called *chorofýlakes*. You'll recognize them by their green uniforms. (POLICE is written on the doors of patrol cars.)

The *Touristikí Astynomía* (tourist police) are a separate branch of the police force whose job it is to help foreign visitors in distress. The distinctive patches (national flags) sewn on their blue uniforms indicate foreign languages spoken. The tourist police have the authority to inspect prices in restaurants and hotels. If you've a complaint, these are the people to see. To get in touch with them, inquire at any tourist information office.

Where's the nearest police station?	**Pou íne to kodinótero astynomikó tmíma?**

POST OFFICE (ΤΑΧΥΔΡΟΜΕΙΟ—*tachydromío*). Post offices handle stamp sales, parcels and money orders within Greece, but not telephone calls or telegrams; see TELEGRAMS AND TELEPHONE.

Post offices in the larger towns on the island can be recognized by a yellow sign reading ΕΛ.ΤΑ. In Ágios Nikólaos the post office is located on Neapóleos; in Chaniá on Odós Tzanakáki; in Iráklion on Platía Daskalogiánni; in Réthimnon on Th. Moatsu. See also HOURS.

Stamps can also be purchased at news-stands and souvenir shops, but at a 10 per cent surcharge. Letter boxes are painted yellow.

P   The post office clerk is obliged to check the contents of any registered letters as well as of parcels addressed to foreign destinations, so don't seal this kind of mail until it has been "approved".

express (special delivery)	**exprés**
airmail	**aeroporikós**
registered	**systiméno**
poste restante (general delivery)	**poste-restante**
A stamp for this letter/postcard, please.	**Éna grammatósimo giaftó to grámma/kart postál, parakaló.**

PUBLIC HOLIDAYS *(argíes)*. The following civil and religious holidays are observed throughout Greece when banks, offices and shops are closed:

Jan. 1	*Protochroniá*	New Year's Day
Jan. 6	*ton Theofaníon*	Epiphany
March 25	*Ikostí Pémti Martíou (tou Evangelismoú)*	Greek Independence Day
May 1	*Protomagiá*	May Day
Aug. 15	*Dekapendávgoustos (tis Panagías)*	Assumption Day
Oct. 28	*Ikostí Ogdóï Oktovríou*	Óchi ("No") Day, commemorating Greek defiance of Italian ultimatum and invasion of 1940
Dec. 25	*Christoúgenna*	Christmas Day
Dec. 26	*défteri iméra ton Christougénnon*	St. Stephen's Day
Movable dates:	*Katharí Deftéra*	1st Day of Lent: Clean Monday
	Megáli Paraskeví	Good Friday
	Deftéra tou Páscha	Easter Monday
	Análipsis	Ascension
	tou Agíou Pnévmatos	Whit Monday ("Holy Spirit")

Note: The dates on which the movable holy days are celebrated often differ from those in Catholic and Protestant countries.

Are you open tomorrow?	**Échete aniktá ávrio?**

RADIO and TV *(rádio; tileórasi)*. News in English is broadcast every day on local Greek radio and TV. ERT-4, the Armed Forces Radio, also broadcasts the news daily in English. In addition, with a good transistor radio, you'll be able to pick up the BBC World Service and the Voice of America very clearly in the evening and early morning.

Almost all hotels on the island have TV lounges (unfortunately so do many *tavérnes* and restaurants). Many of the programmes are imported, well-known TV series in English with Greek subtitles, while a good percentage of the local programmes are musical.

TAXIS (ΤΑΞΙ—*taxí*). Despite high fuel prices, taxis remain quite cheap on Crete. The drivers are generally helpful and honest.

Taxis are plentiful in the towns, and you should have no problem finding one—the streets are generally full of cruising cabs. They carry a sign reading either ΤΑΞΙ or Taxi on their roofs. There are also taxi ranks where the taxis, not the customers, have to queue up. Almost every village has at least one taxi, which isn't surprising since few villagers own their own cars. These rural taxis are called *agoréon* (ΑΓΟΡΑΙΟΝ).

Don't feel you're being cheated if, at the end of the trip, the taxi driver adds a surcharge to the fare at Easter and Christmas; this surcharge is quite legitimate. As a tip, taxi drivers expect you to round off the fare. To show your appreciation for special services rendered, you might nevertheless like to give a little extra.

What's the fare to...? **Piá íne i timí giá...?**

TELEGRAMS and TELEPHONE *(tilegráfima; tiléfono)*. Each major town on Crete has an office of Greece's telecommunications organization (OTE), open 6 a.m. to midnight daily. Many smaller towns and villages also have OTE offices, but hours are shorter (usually 7.30 a.m. to 10 p.m., Monday to Friday). Here you can send telegrams, and dial by yourself or have an operator obtain telephone numbers. You can also make a local call from phone booths on the street or from news-stands. Telephones which are linked to the international dialling system carry a large "Telephone" sign, with instructions in English given inside the booth. You'll need a supply of 5-, 10- and 20- (sometimes 50-) drachma pieces.

Greece's telephone system has direct dialling facilities to many countries around the world. Nevertheless, international trunk lines are often busy, and it may be advisable to place your call through the operator. Your hotel receptionist will take care of that for you.

T

At peak traffic times, you may have to wait for up to two hours for your connection.

I want to send a telegram to…	**Thélo na stílo éna tilegráfima sto…**
Can you get me this number in…?	**Boríte na mou párete aftó ton arithmó…?**

TIME DIFFERENCES. The chart below shows the time differences between Greece and some selected cities.

Los Angeles	Chicago	New York	London	**Crete**
2 a.m.	4 a.m.	5 a.m.	10 a.m.	**noon**

In winter, Greek clocks are turned back one hour. If your country does the same, the difference in time remains the same as in summer.

What time is it?	**Ti óra íne?**

TIPPING. By law, service charges are included in the bill at hotels, restaurants and *tavérnes*. The Greeks aren't tip-crazy, but they do expect you to leave a little more—if the service has been good, of course.

Even if your room or meals are included as part of a package tour, you'll still want to remember the maid and the waiter. The waiter will probably have a *mikró* (an assistant, or busboy), who should get a token of appreciation as well.

Hotel porter, per bag	30–50 drs.
Maid, per day	100 drs.
Waiter	5% (optional)
Taxi driver	10% (optional)
Tour guide (½ day)	100–200 drs. (optional)
Hairdresser/Barbers	10%
Lavatory attendant	20 drs.

TOILETS (ΤΟΥΑΛΕΤΤΕΣ—*toualéttes*). All the towns on the north coast of the island have public toilets. They are located near the general markets or in the parks. In villages, try a café or *tavérna* (it's considered polite to have a coffee or some other drink if you drop in specifically to use the facilities). ΓΥΝΑΙΚΩΝ means "ladies" and ΑΝΔΡΩΝ, "gentlemen".

Where are the toilets?	**Pou íne i toualéttes?**

TOURIST INFORMATION OFFICES *(grafío pliroforión tourismoú).* The following branches of the Greek National Tourist Organization *(Ellinikós Organismós Tourismoú,* abbreviated EOT) will supply you with a wide range of colourful and informative brochures and maps in English. They will also let you consult the master directory of hotels in Greece, listing all facilities and prices.

British Isles: 195–7, Regent St., London WIR 8DL; tel.: (01) 734-5997

U.S.A.: 645 5th Ave., New York, NY 10022; tel.: (212) 421-5777; 611 W. 6th St., Los Angeles, CA 90017; tel.: (213) 626-6696
168 N. Michigan Ave., Chicago, IL 60601; tel. (312) 782-1084.

Canada: 80 Bloor St. West, Suite 1403, Toronto, Ont. M5S 2V1;
tel. (416) 968-2220.
1233, rue de la Montagne, Montreal, Que. H3G 1Z2;
tel. (514) 871-1532.

On Crete itself, tourist information offices are located in the main towns. They all keep the same hours: 7.30 a.m. to 7.30 p.m. (2.30 p.m. Sundays and holidays). The sign over the door reads EOT.

Iráklion: Across from the Archaeological Museum; tel.: 228-203 or 228-225

Réthimnon: On the seafront promenade; tel.: 29-148 or 24-143

Chaniá: In the Mosque of the Janissaries on the harbour; tel.: 26-426

Ágios Nikólaos: K. Paleológou 17; tel.: 23-333

Where's the tourist office?	**Pou íne to grafío tourismoú?**

WATER *(neró).* Tap water is almost always safe to drink (though if it comes unfiltered from a water tank you may prefer to order bottled water). In a Greek café or restaurant you'll usually be served a glass of water as a chaser for alcoholic drinks and coffee.

a bottle of mineral water	**éna boukáli metallikó neró**
fizzy (carbonated)/still	**me/chorís anthrakikó**
Is this drinking water?	**Íne pósimo aftó to neró?**

DAYS OF THE WEEK

Sunday	**Kyriakí**	Thursday	**Pémti**
Monday	**Deftéra**	Friday	**Paraskeví**
Tuesday	**Tríti**	Saturday	**Sávvato**
Wednesday	**Tetárti**		

MONTHS

January	**Ianouários**	July	**Ioúlios**
February	**Fevrouários**	August	**Ávgoustos**
March	**Mártios**	September	**Septémvrios**
April	**Aprílios**	October	**Októvrios**
May	**Máios**	November	**Noémvrios**
June	**Ioúnios**	December	**Dekémvrios**

NUMBERS

0	**midén**	18	**dekaoktó**
1	**éna**	19	**dekaenniá**
2	**dío**	20	**íkosi**
3	**tría**	21	**íkosi éna**
4	**téssera**	22	**íkosi dío**
5	**pénde**	30	**triánda**
6	**éxi**	31	**triánda éna**
7	**eptá**	40	**saránda**
8	**októ**	50	**penínda**
9	**enniá**	60	**exínda**
10	**déka**	70	**evdomínda**
11	**éndeka**	80	**ogdónda**
12	**dódeka**	90	**enenínda**
13	**dekatría**	100	**ekató**
14	**dekatéssera**	101	**ekatón éna**
15	**dekapénde**	102	**ekatón dío**
16	**dekaéxi**	500	**pendakósia**
17	**dekaeptá**	1,000	**chília**

SOME USEFUL EXPRESSIONS

yes/no	**ne/óchi**
please/thank you	**parakaló/efcharistó**
excuse me/you're welcome	**me sinchoríte/típota**
where/when/how	**pou/póte/pos**
how long/how far	**póso keró/póso makriá**
yesterday/today/tomorrow	**chthes/símera/ávrio**
day/week/month/year	**iméra/evdomáda/mínas/chrónos**
left/right	**aristerá/dexiá**
up/down	**epáno/káto**
good/bad	**kalós/kakós**
big/small	**megálos/mikrós**
cheap/expensive	**ftinós/akrivós**
hot/cold	**zestós/kríos**
old/new	**paliós/néos**
open/closed	**aniktós/klistós**
Is there anyone here who speaks English?	**Íne kanís edó na milá i angliká?**
I don't understand.	**Den katalavéno.**
Please write it down.	**Parakaló grápste to.**
What does this mean?	**Ti siméni aftó?**
What time is it?	**Ti óra íne?**
How much is that?	**Póso káni aftó?**
I'd like...	**Tha íthela...**
Where are the toilets?	**Pou íne i toualéttes?**
Waiter, please!	**Parakaló!**
Can you help me, please?	**Voïthíste me, parakaló.**
Call a doctor—quickly!	**Kaléste éna giatró—grígora!**
What do you want?	**Ti thélete?**
Just a minute.	**Éna leptó.**
Go away!	**Fígete!**

Index

An asterisk (*) next to a page number indicates a map reference. For index to Practical Information, see inside front cover.

Abu Hafs Omar 18
Agía Galíni 44, 54*
Agía Rouméli 54*, 66
Agía Triáda 31, 32, 40, 43, 54*
Ágios Geórgios 46*, 68
Ágios Nikólaos 46*, 47, 49
Agrími (kri-kri) 64, 86–87
Akrotíri 54*, 61
Anógia 54*, 69, 70, 80
Ariadne 14–15
Arsenali
 Chaniá 57*, 58
 Iráklion 26

Barbarossa 20, 51
Basilicas—see Churches
Battle of Crete 22, 62
Beaches 10, 23, 32, 44, 51, 52, 56, 59, 61, 82–83
Boating 80–81
Bougátsa 28, 89
Bouzoúki 73
Bull-leaping 13–14, 15, 39
Buses 26, 56, 61, 64, 69, 103–4

Candia 19, 20
Chaniá 10, 20, 23, 54*, 57*, 56–61, 74
Chanióporta 25*, 26
Chóra Sfakíon 54*, 61–62, 67
Chrisoskalítissa (nunnery) 62
Churches
 Ágia Ekateríni (Iráklion) 19, 25*, 29
 Ágios Frangískos (Chaniá) 57*, 58
 Ágios Márkos (Iráklion) 25*, 28–29
 Ágios Minás (Iráklion) 29
 Ágios Nikólaos (Chaniá) 57*, 59
 Ágios Títos (Iráklion) 25*, 29
 Panagiá Kerá (Kritsá) 46*, 49
Climate 10, 47, 50, 99
Code of Laws (Górtis) 18, 40

Daedalus 14, 35
Damaskinós, Michaïl 19, 29
Dances 73
Día Island 24, 46*
Diktaean Cave 46*, 49, 67–68, 69
Díkti, Mount 8, 40, 46*, 67–68
Dittany 57, 64, 86
Dorians 17, 40

Elafonísi Islands 54*, 70
El Greco 19, 29, 53
El Greco Park (Iráklion) 25*, 29
Eloúnda 46*, 69, 82
Énosis 21–22
Europa 8
Evans, Arthur 6–7, 12–13, 16, 22, 32, 35–36
Evréïka quarter (Chaniá) 57* 60

Falásarna 54*, 62
Fauna 64, 86–87
Festivals 51, 55, 73–75
Festós, see Phaistós
Firkás (Chaniá) 57*, 58

Fishing 82
Flora 32, 64–65, 84–86
Fódele 46*, 53
Folklore 51, 73–74
Food 30, 88–96
Fortétza (Réthimnon) 55
Frangokástello 54*, 62

Gávdos 54*, 62
George, Prince 21
Germans 22, 44, 62
Gioúktas, Mount 35
Górtis (Górtina) 18, 40, 46*
Goulás 49
Gourniá 46*, 49–50

Harbours
  Chaniá 57*, 58–59
  Iráklion 24
Hiking 67, 84
Homer 6, 12, 69

Icons 29, 52
Idaian Cave 54*, 69
Ídi, Mount 8, 40, 54*, 68–69
Ierápetra 46*, 49, 50, 79
Iráklion 10, 19, 21, 23, 24–32, 25*, 46*

Kafenío 93
Kalí Liménes 18
Kalokairinós, Mínos 32
Kamáres 54*, 69
Karzános 71
Kastélli Kissámou 54*, 62
Kastélli quarter (Chaniá) 57*, 59
Káto Zákros 6, 31, 46*, 51–52
Kazantzákis, Níkos 20, 26, 32
Knossós 6, 12, 16, 22, 23, 32–39, 33*, 46*, 75
Kornáros, Ioánnis 52
Kornáros, Vitsénzos 19

Koúles—see Venetian Castle
Kourná, Lake 54*, 56
Kritsá 46*, 49, 80
Kydonía 59

Labyrinth 7, 14–15, 35
Language 16, 24, 96, 115
La Parisienne 14, 31
Lasíthi Plains 46*, 49, 67
Lató 46*, 49
Limín Chersonísou 45, 46*
Lýra 73

Máleme 54*, 62
Mália 6, 31, 45, 46*
Markets
  Chaniá 57*, 57
  Iráklion 29
Mátala 40, 44, 54*
Messará Plain 7, 40, 46*
Mezé 93–94
Miller, Henry 40
Minoans 6–8, 12–16, 35, 39, 42–44, 66, 68
Minos, King 12, 14, 35
Minotaur 14–15
Mirabéllo Bay 46*, 47, 81, 82
Móchlos Island 46*, 70, 74, 82
Monasteries
  Agía Triáda 54*, 61
  Arkádi 54*, 56, 74
  Gouvernétou 61
  Katholikó 61
  Préveli 53, 54*
  Toploú 46*, 52
Morosini Fountain (Iráklion) 27–28
Mosques
  Janissaries (Chaniá) 57*, 58
  Neranziés (Réthimnon) 55
Museums 75–76
  Archaeological (Chaniá) 57*, 58

INDEX

INDEX

Museums (cont.)
  Archaeological (Iráklion) 23, 25*, 30–32, 47, 75–76
  Archaeological (Réthimnon) 56
  Historical (Iráklion) 25*, 32, 76
  Naval (Chaniá) 57*, 58

Neápolis 46*, 47, 74, 90
Nída Plain 69

Odyssey 6, 12, 62, 69
Oloús 46*, 70, 82
Omalós 54*, 64
Oúzo 93, 96

Paleochóra 54*, 62, 67
Paul, St. 18
Phaistós (Festós) 6, 7, 40, 42–43, 44, 54*, 75
Phaistós Disc 16, 17, 31, 43
Píthoi 36, 43
Platía
  Eleftherías (Iráklion) 25*, 30
  Venizélou (Iráklion) 25*, 26
Polyrrinía 54*, 62
Profítis Ilías 46*, 54*, 61
Promachón Martinéngo (Iráklion) 26
Psíra Island 46*, 70
Psichró 46*, 67

Rabd-el-Kandek 18–19
Restaurants 30, 90–92
Réthimnon 10, 20, 23, 53–56, 54*
Riviera of Crete 10, 51
Romans 8, 18, 40

Samariá, Gorge of 54*, 64–66, 87
Saracen Arabs 8, 18–19

Schliemann, Heinrich 32
Sfakiá Mountains 10, 61, 90
Sfakiotes 10, 61–62
Sfinári 62
Shopping 76–80
Sitía 46*, 51
Skin-diving 82
Soúda Bay 54*, 56
Soúgia 62, 67
Soumáda 47, 90
Spíli 53, 54*
Spinalónga Island 46*, 49, 69–70
Sports—see individual listings
Swimming 82–83
Synikía Topanás (Chaniá) 57*, 59–60

Tárra 66
Tavérnes 72, 73, 93
Tennis 25*, 83
Theotokópoulos, Domínikos—see El Greco
Theseus 14–15
Throne room (Knossós) 36
Turks 8, 19–22, 29, 35, 56, 70

Váï 46*, 52
Váthi 62
Venetians 8, 19–20, 24, 58, 66
Venetian Castle (Iráklion) 24, 25*
Venetian Walls (Iráklion) 25*, 26
Venizélos, Eleftherios 21, 61
Vólta 30, 56, 92
Voulisméni Lake 47, 49
Vourvoulíti Pass 40

Water-skiing 81
Windmills 48–49
Wine 55, 95–96

Zeus 8, 24, 49, 67, 68, 69